"All of us struggle with life's challenges and develop addictions to some degree. It takes great awareness to truly overcome these pitfalls, which serve as either a path to self-destruction or self-development. Peter Amato has skillfully used his own life experiences, both successes and failures, to illustrate both possibilities. In this insightful self-analysis, he applies the yogic approach to the 12 Steps, creating an even larger opportunity, which is moving from Recovery to Self-Discovery. It is only through contemplative prayer—meditation—that the silent knowledge of the true Self is revealed. Conscious contact brings us to the level of our soul's reality. In that moment, we are not thinking about God, but we are being one with God, directly experiencing the oneness with God. Actualizing Him in each moment of our lives."

—**Yogi Amrit Desai**

"What truly amazes me about Peter Amato is not the extreme metamorphosis he has undergone as a human being, but rather the fact that he can remember all of the insanity leading up to the cocoon stage of his transformation. I have trouble remembering the nineties, let alone what I was or wasn't doing. Peter's *Soul Silence* is an absolute must for anyone who wishes to experience the 12-Step model and not just read about it. His brand of teaching will benefit all those in recovery and the people who care about them."

—**Darren Kavinoky**, TV legal analyst,
founding attorney of the Kavinoky Law Firm

"Peter Amato's *Soul Silence* offers an intimate and beautiful journey of surrender and self-awareness, a guide to living with higher purpose and promise a day at a time. Peter has created a wonderful written companion for the 12-Step person looking to incorporate meditation and yoga into their wholesome design for living."

—**Tian Dayton, Ph.D.**, TEP, author of *Emotional Sobriety: From Relationship Trauma to Resilience and Balance* and creator of RTR: Relationship Trauma Repair Model: Healing PTSD

"Peter has selflessly devoted many years to study with many masters. The result is a valuable gift for the recovery community."

—**Gary Seidler**, founding copublisher of Health Communications, Inc.

"Fostering strong spiritual health is paramount to recovery. In my experience with recovering addicts, individuals who establish and maintain a strong spiritual connection have a much better chance of staying sober. Peter Amato's "Soul Silence" is one of the few books I've had the pleasure of reading that not only explains the importance of spiritual healing but also teaches the reader how to develop a deeper connection."

—**Dr. Reef Karim**, director of the Control Center, UCLA Assistant Clinical Professor

"Peter Amato's story is both a cautionary tale and an evolutionary journey into the heart of recovery's most subtle, intangible step— the step that lasts a lifetime. Mr. Amato reveals the beauty and necessity of practicing Step 11. Prayer and meditation's importance to a healthy and successful recovery is explained in an eloquent and down-to-earth fashion. *Soul Silence* is not only a guide, but also a book that explains to every reader how they can create an openness, which allows inspiration and transformation to take place."

—**Leonard Buschell**, founder of Writers in Treatment and the Reel Recovery Film Festival

"Peter Amato's *Soul Silence* is an enlightened guide to self-discovery for the individual in recovery or anyone searching for a deeper connection with themselves. His journey is compelling, and his ability to extract the teachable moments along the way is truly profound."

—**Sophie Chiche**, founder and president of lifebyme.com

"For those individuals in a 12-step program of recovery, it is paramount to maintain a spiritual connection with some form of higher power. While this is a daunting task for many, Peter Amato's *Soul Silence* is a beautifully written guide for anyone to follow when searching for a deeper connection to the 12 Steps and beyond. Through Peter's own down-to-earth experience, strength, and hope, he demystifies the process of connecting to a power greater than yourself."

—**Joan Borysenko, Ph.D.**, author of *It's Not the End of the World: Developing Resilience in Times of Change*

"Peter adds to the unarguable evidence that discovering, aligning, and communing with our true soul-nature is the most seductive of all allures. His wisdom-guided teachings apply to any form of addiction, but especially to that which is the most pervasive of all others: the ego's addiction to a sense of being separate from our Source."

—**Michael Bernard Beckwith**, author of *Spiritual Liberation: Fulfilling Your Soul's Potential*

"We know that recovery is dependent on a spiritual experience that rests upon a pedestal of hopelessness. The question that therefore needs to be answered is, "What can I do to facilitate that spiritual experience?" There are many roads that lead to this transformation; Peter has illuminated one of them. He not only helps us understand the principles underlying his approach but also gives us practical suggestions along the way. These are the hallmarks of a good healer and guide. I am certain that *Soul Silence* will help many people in recovery begin and eventually integrate a daily spiritual practice in their program."

—**Allen Berger, Ph.D.**, author of the recovery mainstay
12 Stupid Things that Mess Up Recovery and
12 Smart Things to Do When the Booze and Drugs Are Gone

SOUL SILENCE

A UNIQUE APPROACH TO MASTERING THE 11TH STEP

PETER AMATO, M.A.

Health Communications, Inc.
Deerfield Beach, Florida

www.hcibooks.com

Library of Congress Cataloging-in-Publication Data

Amato, Peter.
    Soul silence : a unique approach to mastering the eleventh step / Peter Amato.
        p.   cm.
    Includes index.
    ISBN-13: 978-0-7573-1530-5
    ISBN-10: 0-7573-1530-5
    1. Meditation. 2. Twelve-step programs. 3. Compulsive behavior—Treatment.
    4. Self-help techniques. I. Title.
    BL627.A436 2010
    616.86'10652—dc22
                                                                    2010031236

Publisher: Health Communications, Inc.
        3201 S.W. 15th Street
        Deerfield Beach, FL 33442–8190

Cover design by Justin Rothkowitz
Interior design and formatting by Lawna Patterson Oldfield

To my students and
anyone who seeks a deeper
understanding of the narrow,
twisted dream of ordinary
consciousness.

IN THE ATTITUDE OF SILENCE THE

SOUL FINDS THE PATH IN A CLEARER LIGHT,

AND WHAT IS ELUSIVE AND DECEPTIVE

RESOLVES ITSELF INTO CRYSTAL CLEARNESS.

—*Mahatma Gandhi*

CONTENTS

PART THREE: **Peace, Passion, and Purpose**

FOREWORD

Step 11

Sought through prayer and meditation to improve our conscious contact with God, as we understood Him, praying only for knowledge of His will for us and the power to carry that out.

Let me begin by saying that a mere 58,895 hours ago I was what substance abusers like to call a *Hope to Die* addict. I'm sure it sounds like a dramatic title to some, but I can assure you, it is a simple and profoundly accurate description of my frame of mind at that time.

Like many addicts and alcoholics out there, I hoped for death every day, with every hit, with every line, with every thought, but didn't have the courage to take my own life, so I enlisted the help of drugs and alcohol to do the job. For most people, reading words like "take my own life" and "courage" in the same sentence is preposterous and they'd be right, but that type of thinking is indicative of how warped the mind of an addict becomes with enough abuse and isolation.

Contrary to popular belief, the mind of an addict is highly active, which makes the existence of an addict quite a debilitating conundrum. In essence, addicts want to feel different for whatever reason so they use a substance that initially makes them feel good. They want to feel good again, so they repeatedly use and soon abuse that substance. Their entire beings are reprogrammed and now, in order to feel normal, they must use the substance constantly or they will become emotionally and physically sick. At this point, when the mind reaches a tipping point, death seems like the only way out. A *Hope to Die* addict is born, one who still dreams of feeling good, which keeps the cycle moving, but who truly believes that death is the only hope for change.

Now, before you flip the page and head right for the main content, I must let you know that this is the most important foreword you will ever read. That may seem grandiose, but it has nothing to do with my writing and everything to do with the fact that the book you are about to read is, in my humble opinion, the most important literary work thus far that teaches addicts and virtually anyone how to not just learn to follow the literal and figurative steps toward recovery, but also *experience* each step in a way that until now hasn't been written about or taught.

I am an average individual whose only diploma comes from the school of hard knocks and whose only qualification as an addiction expert comes from experience as a full-blown addict. I regularly attend AA meetings and have roughly seven years of sobriety, which blows my mind. After many years of abuse, I was given the gift of treatment and made my way off the streets. The first thing I found was an amazing AA group and never looked back. I did what I was told and followed one of my favorite AA directions of all time: *fake it 'till you make it.*

If you immerse yourself very early on and climb those steps diligently, you'll find that the answers to all of your questions are in the rooms of AA. Whether on the pages of a big blue book or from the wisdom of others, everything you need to live an incredible life is in those rooms. It was only recently that I realized there had to be more than simply finding solace in the words. Now I have to be careful—I am not saying that the answers are not in those words, I am saying that my personal experience brought me to a place where I was feeling disconnected from the words and was looking for a new way to connect with the solution.

It is difficult enough to articulate that feeling to a friend or sponsor but I had to, so I began asking people if they could relate to what I was, or perhaps wasn't, feeling. While many people feel ignorance is bliss and rocking the boat with questions like mine is dangerous, I knew in my heart the answer was out there . . . and it was.

One morning while I was reading through a *daily readings* book, waiting for my AA meeting to start, an individual I'd seen around sporadically sat down beside me and handed me what looked like a tattered manuscript barely bound by one giant clip in the corner. He proceeded to tell me that he'd overheard me talking to a few people and felt like I might find what I was looking for on those pages.

It was, in fact, a manuscript. It was a very early version of Peter Amato's *Soul Silence: A Unique Approach to Mastering the 11th Step.* I was told to show it to no one and to return it in a week. It all seemed a little bizarre to me, but I have eaten food out of trash cans, so I think I can read something a stranger suggests.

Now, I've read and said the 11th Step a million times, but something profound happened to me the moment I began reading Peter's book; I began to see beyond the words and actually experience the message contained in that step and the other eleven. This was exactly what I was looking for—a beautifully written book intended to make my recovery an experiential process.

For me, it was the difference between recovery VHS and recovery Blu-ray. Everything I had learned to date was the same, but Peter showed me how to see and experience the process at a higher level of awareness. I wasn't reading the steps; I *was* the steps. My spiritual connection with my higher power was no longer an idea; it was a feeling that took my idea of connection to a place I could never have imagined.

I read all 288 pages in one sitting, and I've never been the same since. Everything changed in a matter of hours, and I remember wanting to share it with everyone who would listen. I felt like it was such a significant gift that I needed to return it as soon as possible and find out where I could get a copy of my own. I walked into my meeting the next day and shared a powerful moment with the person who gave it to me. Neither one of us said a word, but the look we exchanged carried a sense of comfort and understanding I've never experienced before. This was a special gift, and I needed to share it with everyone.

All I could muster was, "Where can I buy a copy?" My new friend only laughed and told me he couldn't tell me where he got the draft, but it was definitely going to be available soon. I immediately began researching Peter Amato and realized that while he is close with people like Andrew Weil and Deepak Chopra, he is about the coolest individual out there and has an "everyman" quality that just makes me feel better about everything.

I reached out to him directly to share my experience and was fortunate to have a few exchanges with him over the phone. Peter can discuss everything from car racing to enlightenment and it all feels spiritual. At the end of our last conversation he asked me if I'd like to write the foreword to his book, and after I picked my chin up off of the floor, I asked, "Why not have one of your incredible peers write something that important?" He replied in his calm voice, "I am."

I will never forget that exchange or the fact that Peter Amato and this book have opened up a connection to myself and my higher power that have not only added a touch of enlightenment to my recovery, but have also proven there is a deeper connection to everything, and *Soul Silence* is my conduit. Let it be yours.

—Rob A.

ACKNOWLEDGMENTS

WHEN WE PRAY AND MEDITATE we gain the important insight that we are all inextricably linked to our universe and one another. In that spirit, I want to thank Gary Seidler, Peter Vegso, and Michele Matrisciani for recognizing that my life's journey and my experience as a meditation and yoga teacher would translate into a book that serves the recovery community in a new way. I also thank my editor Carol Rosenberg for her enthusiasm for this material and her keen editorial eye.

I express deep gratitude to June Frushon for her tireless work, love, and support; Sheila McDonald for her extensive contributions to the yoga section of this book; and Steve Szydlowski for keeping me grounded in earthly matters. I also thank Brian Zywicki and Suzi Welebob for their assistance with the yoga photography on these pages. I want to acknowledge the divine connection I feel with Gina Gold, whose craft and story sense made this book possible.

I thank my higher power and Alcoholics Anonymous for the beautiful gift of sobriety, and my many visionary teachers for showing me that sobriety is only the first step on an amazing path filled with peace, passion, and purpose.

Finally, I express my deepest gratitude to my students, whose brave and incredible journeys from darkness to light have inspired this book and continue to inspire my work as a teacher.

PREFACE

*Sought through prayer and meditation to improve
our conscious contact with God as we understood Him,
praying only for knowledge of His will for us
and the power to carry that out.*

—Eleventh Step of Alcoholics Anonymous

IN 1993, TOWARD THE END of my twenty-eight-day stay in a rehabilitation facility for an ugly alcohol and cocaine addiction, Tom C., a member of Alcoholics Anonymous, paid me a visit. He was a no-nonsense, pragmatic business guy doing some service. He spoke my language. I got him; he got me. He asked why I'd checked in: "What happened?"

I told him that a district attorney had given me an ultimatum: rehab or jail. Not much of a choice. We talked about my business as an auto parts distributor and about my family and friends. He recounted his own battle with addiction and told me how he'd turned his life around one day at a time. The man seemed pretty peaceful so I asked how I could get what he had. Then he uttered a few words that changed my life forever: "Start the Eleventh Step now."

Tom told me to pray and meditate for thirty minutes a day for thirty days. "Don't wait until you've worked through the first ten steps. Start now. Observe your breathing and any time you slip off to a thought, emotion, or feeling simply note it and escort your mind back to the next inhale."

I laughed. Me, pray and meditate? I was a high-energy auto parts guy who spent his days hitting sales targets in the millions. I blew off steam on weekends, drag racing at speeds over 150 miles an hour, getting wasted on alcohol, and snorting cocaine. I'd broken a national drag racing record, for chrissakes. I lived for conversations about race engines, horsepower, chassis length, tire size, transmissions, and rear-end gear ratios. Our business sponsored my brother's drag racing career, helping him land five National Hot Rod Association (NHRA) world championships. Me, meditate? Was he crazy?

But Tom calmly went on, explaining that if I could find it in me to pray and meditate for a month the benefits would be exponential. Not only would I stay sober, my health would improve, my thinking would become clear, and the idea of drinking and drugging would seem ridiculous. If I could sit for thirty minutes every day, my recovery would take a quantum leap forward. While other people were still struggling to stay sober I would find relief and serenity quickly.

Well that clinched it: speed and competition. If I was going to do this damn recovery thing, I was going to do it faster and better than anyone else.

Looking back at that encounter so many years ago, I laugh at my motivation, but I also know that the universe had sent me the perfect messenger, someone who knew exactly what to say to make me listen. Tom later became my sponsor, and I am eternally grateful for his love, support, and guidance. I have been clean and sober—one day at a time—ever since. And he was right. Praying and meditating from the start did much more than keep me sober. I made huge strides in my recovery. Fast. After less than a year of regular prayer and meditation—as I watched friends in the program continue to struggle with people, places, and things—I began to see clearly who I really was and the role I wanted to play in the world. Very little bothered me. I came to understand that my soul—the essence of who I am—never drank or used drugs.

I came in contact with a part of myself that is so pure and untouchable nothing can destroy it. Eventually, the peace I experienced was so profound that the idea of drinking or using drugs became beside the point—just as my sponsor had promised. I came to see that the spiritual connection I had been seeking had been within me all along; I'd just never been able to sit still long enough to feel it.

Today, I am a certified meditation and yoga instructor and a transpersonal psychotherapist. I am also president and CEO of a chain of groundbreaking integrative medical centers, a yoga school, and an educational outreach company specializing in transformational programs. I recently cofounded a cutting-edge outpatient rehabilitation facility and will soon begin my doctoral studies in mind-body medicine.

Today, using a method I call the Inner Harmony Approach, I have taught more than a thousand men and women how to use prayer, meditation, and self-inquiry to deepen and solidify their recovery from addiction to alcohol, drugs, food, sex, debt, gambling, and unhealthy relationships, among other things. That's right, me . . . the car guy. I became what I once would have called *woo woo*.

I'll talk more about this unlikely transformation later, but for now, I offer anyone recovering from addiction a message that is not *woo woo* at all. It is a profoundly simple and practical one; it is the same message given to me so many years ago: Start the Eleventh Step now. Even if you can only manage to sit still for one minute a day: Start now.

INTRODUCTION:
Addiction and the Eleventh Step

*All man's miseries derive from not being
able to sit quietly in a room alone.*

—Blaise Pascal

PRAYER AND MEDITATION ARE as old as the earth's ancient religions, but the idea of using them as part of a systematic program of recovery from addiction is relatively new. In 1935, when alcoholics were routinely locked up in sanitariums and asylums, two physically, emotionally, and spiritually bankrupt alcoholics figured out that admitting complete defeat and asking a higher power *of their understanding* for help was the only way to overcome their addiction.

These pioneers—a businessman named Bill Wilson and a physician named Robert Smith—also understood that the only way they would stay sober was to continually share their message with other alcoholics, ensuring they themselves never forgot to seek a connection to their higher power.

Bill W. and Dr. Bob's small meetings of ragtag alcoholics steadily grew into a fellowship called Alcoholics Anonymous (AA), which, according to the group's World Service Office, now serves about 2 million members at 113,168 meetings in more than 180 countries. AA, a nonprofit, member-run organization, also reports that today scores of offshoots use AA's Twelve Steps and Twelve Traditions as a foundation for helping people recover from addictions of all kinds.

In addition to alcoholism, Twelve Step meetings serve people seeking relief from drug abuse, overeating, anorexia, gambling, codependence, sex addiction, Internet addiction, workaholism, compulsive debting, and chronic hoarding to name a few issues. Even people who are perpetually late and suffer from severe artistic blocks have turned to the Twelve Steps for help.

Making Conscious Contact
with a Higher Power

Most mental health and addiction professionals acknowledge the unparalleled effectiveness of Twelve Step programs, referring clients to "the rooms" for their combination of ongoing peer support, structure, and nondenominational spirituality. It turns out that spirituality—the quest for a connection with something greater than oneself—is a powerful tool that helps free addicts from the grips of addiction.

Why? No one is entirely sure. Some theologians and religious believers say it is the work of God. Some scientists, atheists, and agnostics suggest the Twelve Steps introduce recovering addicts to new ways of thinking—create new mental pathways—that override brain chemistry that has evolved over millennia. And, of course, there are plenty of people whose opinion falls somewhere in the middle.

While it is helpful to explore the reasons *why* the spiritual aspects of the program work, it is more important to understand the fact that they *do* work. Recovery professionals and recovering addicts acknowledge that addicts who connect—that is, make *conscious contact*—with a higher power, however they define it, are more likely to stay sober, abstinent, and serene for longer periods. They move forward in their recovery, not backward. The quality of their lives improves.

Conversely, addicts who struggle to find a meaningful understanding of, and connection with, a higher power are likely to falter in their quest to stay sober or abstinent.

Looking for Clues

I have been blessed to be able to dedicate the past two decades of my life to spiritual inquiry. I have studied with some of the world's greatest spiritual masters, who have imparted powerful and effective tools and techniques for making conscious contact with a higher power of my understanding. I even went so far as to "check out" for seven years so I could meditate and pray with little interruption—that is, until some wise friends convinced me it was time to return to society to give back what I had learned.

So, I made a commitment to service. Since then, scores of men and women in recovery have approached me in my role as a meditation master, yoga teacher, and psychotherapist—some ashamed —saying they haven't a clue how to practice the Eleventh Step. Some can't identify a higher power and others don't know how to connect with the one in which they already believe. Some people have an aversion to any kind of spirituality because they associate it with a particular religious tradition. Others are atheists or agnostics who, without tangible proof, cannot abide the idea of a God or even something as noncommittal as a higher power.

There are those in recovery who have studied meditation, but the techniques they learned didn't resonate with them, or they just can't sit still long enough to experience the miraculous healing these practices can bring. As one AA member put it: "When you walk into a meeting, no one hands you a manual explaining how to do this stuff."

Of course, that is not entirely true. Bill Wilson includes material on prayer and meditation in *Alcoholics Anonymous,* also known as AA's "Big Book." He also wrote an inspired chapter on the subject in the *Twelve Steps and Twelve Traditions* (often called the *Twelve and Twelve*). I strongly encourage you to read both books in their entirety. Furthermore, some Twelve Step programs and publishers specializing in recovery books offer pamphlets about Step Eleven. But there is scant material that explores—in depth—nonreligious, nondenominational ways a person working to overcome addiction can find a higher power and learn to pray and meditate.

Wilson himself acknowledged that when it comes to prayer and meditation, AA itself has its limitations, advising in the *Twelve and Twelve* that AA members seek outside guidance on the matter. "Aided by such instruction and example as we can find, [prayer and meditation are] essentially an individual adventure, something which each one of us works out in his own way."

The Inner Harmony Approach

After watching so many people struggle with prayer and meditation for so long, I felt compelled to share what I had learned. I began offering workshops based on what I call the Inner Harmony Approach to Enlightened Recovery. My approach grew out of the concept that addiction stems from the duality, or split, between the mind and spirit; that the root of addiction lies not in substances or self-destructive behavior but in the disconnection that emerges over time between our thoughts and actions and our true nature.

We practice the Eleventh Step to realign ourselves with this true nature—to achieve inner harmony. Why? Because when we find inner harmony, there is no reason to return to addictive behavior. No high can ever be as satisfying or compelling as a feeling of wholeness. Achieving inner harmony, however, takes some work and commitment. It requires opening your mind and heart to a source of knowledge and strength within, even if that source seems abstract or elusive. If you already have a clear picture of God or a higher power, achieving inner harmony can mean rethinking your relationship to that divine spirit. Wherever you are in your recovery, finding inner harmony depends on your willingness to connect with a source, God, or higher power of your understanding on a regular basis.

So, where do you begin? I can talk about the importance of connecting with a higher power forever, but the best way to understand this connection is to experience it on a deep level. And that requires some skill, some mastery. It's no surprise many people struggle with the Eleventh Step. Prayer and meditation can be confusing practices to grasp, especially when you're left to figure them out on your own.

I created the Inner Harmony workshops to teach men and women—even those without any spiritual or religious bent—the skills they need to practice the Eleventh Step. I offer simple, concrete techniques for practicing prayer and meditation daily so students can discover a higher power of their understanding and connect with it at any time.

If you struggle with the Eleventh Step, be assured that you, like my students, can find a way to practice prayer and meditation that works with your beliefs, your lifestyle, and even your physical and emotional limitations. You can identify and connect with a higher power of your understanding, whether you are devoutly religious, have only a vague idea of a higher power, or are a staunch atheist who is not interested in relying on anyone or anything besides yourself.

What I offer is a method that moves beyond words and intellect, and allows you to sink into deeper states of consciousness where you can experience a higher power inside and around you. All you need is the willingness to try some simple tools for a few minutes a day.

My students who have embraced the techniques in this book report tremendous changes in their lives—new thought patterns, new motivation, and a whole new way of living. If you are willing to do the same, beginning right where you are, you can experience these changes for yourself.

Who Is This Book For?

If you are recovering from addiction or are affected by it, you will find help on these pages. Anyone who attends Twelve Step meetings, including Alcoholics Anonymous, Narcotics Anonymous, Overeaters Anonymous, Gamblers Anonymous, Debtors Anonymous, Al-Anon, Adult Children of Alcoholics, or any program that uses AA's Twelve Steps as a basis for relief from addiction or self-destructive behavior, will find useful ideas and helpful techniques here.

This book is for you if you are newly sober and/or abstinent and can't fathom sitting still long enough to practice the Eleventh Step. It can also serve as a guide for someone who has a few years of recovery but feels stuck in his or her spiritual growth. It is certainly a useful book for "old-timers" seeking to deepen their spiritual practice and renew a commitment to recovery and service.

Most important, this book is for anyone at risk of losing his or her sobriety or abstinence, especially if life feels too overwhelming without the numbing effects of a substance or self-destructive behavior. If you are currently active in your addiction and have some inkling that you have a problem, this book is a beginning, but I strongly urge you to consult the Resources section at the back of this book where you can find help through Twelve Step programs and many other avenues of recovery.

If you are a mental health professional or addiction specialist, you will also find useful information, tools, and techniques between these covers. The practices outlined here can help you teach clients who struggle with substance abuse, process addictions, relationship obsessions, and so on to stay grounded and committed to recovery. If you feel overwhelmed by the tremendous stress and responsibility associated with your noble work, you will certainly find a few techniques here to help yourself.

Simply put, anyone dealing with or affected by addiction and destructive behavior can benefit by reading this book. Herein lie invaluable tools for quieting the mind, connecting to inner wisdom, and finding peace.

Many of the terms, expressions, and ideas in this book will be familiar to people who attend Twelve Step meetings, but I have done my best to define them for people who do not. I also refer to many of the so-called slogans that are popular at meetings. If you are unfamiliar with the sayings or if they seem trite, please keep an open mind about the messages they convey. There are years of accumulated wisdom behind them. Overall, you do not have to be "in the program" to benefit from the information offered in this book. You can belong to a particular religious faith or not; you can be an atheist or agnostic. The underlying tools and techniques offered here are universal.

Finally, writing about spirituality for people with a broad range of religious, philosophical, and social beliefs, can be challenging. Please know that I've taken great pains to be sensitive to people of different religious and nonreligious backgrounds. Nevertheless, I realize that no matter how careful I am, I might offend someone by discussing God or a higher power in a way that feels uncomfortable or inappropriate. Please know this is not my intention, merely a result of my own limitations. Ultimately, this is a book about finding and connecting to a higher power *of your understanding,* so I ask again that you keep an open mind as you consider the ideas in the coming chapters. If something does not resonate for you, please try to ignore it without losing the benefit of other information that might be helpful to your understanding of the Eleventh Step and your journey through recovery.

A Note to Twelve Steppers

This book in no way seeks to replace Alcoholics Anonymous or to contradict anything suggested by its steps, principles, or literature. AA saved my life! This is simply a guide to the "individual adventure" of prayer and meditation that Bill Wilson so wisely suggested you take.

PART ONE:

Stepping into
Step Eleven

1

From Drag Racer to Meditator: My Story

Those whom we call addicts are simply intense seekers of bliss who have gotten stuck in repetition looking for the right thing in the wrong place.

—Yogi Amrit Desai

IT WAS A WARM MAY NIGHT, perfect for barhopping. I screeched my Mercedes into the parking lot of a local dive and swaggered in, twitching from cocaine and blowing my nose into a handkerchief pulled from the pocket of my $10,000 Armani suit. I slammed back one vodka after another as I watched a lounge singer struggle to entertain her chattering audience. I sipped my drink and listened to the music.

Then, as I lifted the glass to my lips, something came over me. Instead of taking the next sip of my drink, I chucked my glass across the room as hard as I could, watching it rocket through the air and slam squarely against the singer's shoulder. Ice and alcohol splattered all over her. The music stopped and everyone glared at me.

At least that's the story I've been told. I don't remember any of it. Not driving there, not the singer, not even being thrown out of the bar. And I have no idea what I had imagined that poor woman had done to make me throw a glass at her.

I found out later that she was upset but unhurt, thank God. But by that point the blackouts had gotten so bad I'd stopped remembering most of the shameful, destructive things I did when I drank and snorted cocaine. What I do remember is that within the next few days a friend approached me with a message from a local district attorney who had caught wind of my frequent and violent bar fights in our tight-knit community. He sent an ultimatum: either I check into a rehabilitation facility on Monday morning or I could expect a police escort to jail on Monday afternoon. For the first time during my mindless, ego-driven spiral downward I was really scared. Scared for myself, scared for my wife and small child. Just scared. My choice was clear.

I entered a rehab located only a few minutes from my home, but found myself a world away from everything I knew. I looked around at the seventy or eighty strangers detoxing with me and thought, *Wow, these people* really *have problems. What am I doing here?*

I collected Ferraris and Lamborghinis. I owned a private jet. I wore hand-tailored suits, and at the age of thirty-eight, I was among the most successful businessmen in my community. I wasn't an addict. Guys under bridges swilling booze from paper bags—*they* were addicts.

So what if I had nine stitches in my head from a previous bar fight? So what if I was under federal investigation after being falsely implicated in a drug ring? So what if my marriage had fallen apart, my little girl barely knew me, and my closest friends were dying from drug addiction? So what if I was jaundiced, sick, and reeling from sorrow so deep I could barely speak? I was nothing like the people in rehab or the guys under the bridge. Not me. I just had an active social life and a very runny nose . . .

The American Nightmare

My descent into hell was driven by money, ambition, and a belief that the American Dream meant absolutely everything. I grew up the youngest child of a working-class family in Scranton, Pennsylvania, a town so renowned for its blue-collar ethics that presidential candidates point to it as the poster child for working-class America. My mother was a loving woman who toiled at home, keeping our household running while my father worked day and night at his automotive parts stores and insisted his children do the same. My dad was a first-generation American whose passion for the American Dream consumed him.

He put me to work at age thirteen, as he had done with my brothers and sister before me. We all worked seven days a week, through our middle school and high school years, every weekend and summer. As the youth-driven revolution of the 1960s and '70s exploded around me, I was busy stocking shelves, mopping floors, and cleaning glass cases, all with the promise of a future filled with money and prestige.

As I was growing up, dinnertime discussions at our house were always about the day's business—purchasing, inventory, sales, and projections. If the company had had a bad day, my father's face would turn red: "What were you thinking?!" he'd yell as he flung plastic fruit off the table.

I was the youngest child, so my father sent me to college to study business. He wanted me to bring important new information back to our growing company. And I did so proudly. Eventually, I left our retail division and was promoted to warehouse duties, phone sales, road sales, purchasing, marketing, and advertising.

Within a few decades, my family's tireless efforts paid off in rapid expansion. My father's single store had grown into twenty-five retail outlets and a worldwide distributorship that employed more than a thousand workers. We operated warehouses from coast to coast with the company's principal facility measuring a mind-boggling one million square feet.

We had financial success most people only dream of. We owned a private jet with pilots on call. I wore the finest handmade clothing and my garage brimmed with exotic sports cars. I competed on the drag racing circuit, thrilled when I broke a national record. Our company sponsored my brother's NHRA drag racing team, which went on to win five world championships, an accomplishment that brought our business even more prestige, credibility, and sales.

Work took me all over the world. Life was fast-paced and thrilling. I loved it. I could snap my fingers and get what I wanted, when I wanted it. I started to believe I was invincible. As sales poured in, I would celebrate with a few drinks and a few more lines of cocaine.

Soon, I relished the release drugs and alcohol brought me from my relentless work and the never-ending push toward the next big deal. I got drunk and high to celebrate the good days and to cry over the bad ones. It never occurred to me there was anything wrong with what I was doing. As far as I was concerned, I was just a recreational partier like everyone else I knew.

Visine and a Handkerchief

But their parties ended and mine never did. I had absolutely everything money could buy, especially drugs and alcohol. I kept drinking and using because I had stopped being able to feel good, not for any real length of time. I was consumed with fear, anxiety, anger, grief, and self-hatred, and I couldn't understand why. I had lived every moment of my life believing financial success and the material things it bought were the key to fulfillment. I finally had everything I had ever worked for, everything I wanted, and there I was twisting in torment.

So, I drank more and did more drugs to numb the pain, especially because I thought I had no one to turn to. I knew most people worked their entire lives to get where I was at such a young age. Who on earth would have compassion for me? Who could possibly believe that someone in my shoes wanted to die?

I grew more and more disillusioned. Soon cocaine became my best friend. In my never-ending quest to be alone with it, I grew more isolated. I pushed away everyone who loved me, including my wife (who had been my high school sweetheart) and our beautiful young daughter.

I worked hard to conceal my ugly secret, making sure I never left home without a handkerchief and Visine to tend to my constantly running nose and watering eyes. Image was so important to me that at one point I hired a professional dresser to label every piece of clothing I owned—matching one to the next. My brain had become so addled that I would pad into my closet hung-over every morning and stare helplessly at my kaleidoscope of imported shirts, ties, suits, and shoes, incapable of figuring out what went with what.

Despite such desperate and deluded attempts to hide my problem, my erratic behavior drew plenty of attention. No one at work had the nerve to say anything because I was the boss. But AA literature would mysteriously show up in my car. I ignored it, of course, since I had no idea what recovery was or that rehabs even existed. My brother, now well aware of my escapades, confronted me. If I didn't have a problem, surely I could stop drinking and using for thirty days.

I tried. *Really tried.* But I couldn't do it.

My façade was cracking. I felt like such a fraud and failure that I would fly into rages. I drank at the most rundown bars I could find because I was sure I belonged there; they were my home. By the time that warm May night rolled around and I so callously hurled my glass across that bar, I was little more than a desperate, lonely addict racing around in a flashy car and an absurdly over-priced suit. I was either incredibly lucky or unlucky that I never got pulled over for a DUI.

A Miraculous Journey

The morning I checked into rehab—"by nudge, grudge, or judge," as they say—I took my first shaky step on a spiritual journey that I can only describe as miraculous. As I struggled through detoxification, the haze lifted and I began to see how utterly powerless I had been over my addiction. I looked around at the men and women in rehab with me, and as I listened to them share their stories—most of them with raw honesty—I saw light return to their eyes.

I yearned for that light to return to my eyes, too. I knew, finally, that I was one of them. I was an alcoholic and an addict. *Just like the guys under the bridge.* It was only by the grace of God and a compassionate district attorney that I was not in jail or dead.

As my twenty-eight days passed, I cried often, filling journal after journal with thoughts and feelings that I had never felt free to express before. I attended AA meetings on site and met regularly with a gifted therapist who explained that long before I had ever turned to drugs and alcohol I had become cut off from my spirit, the essence of my being. She said I was emotionally and spiritually "deadened." Her analysis of my situation struck me as profoundly true.

About three weeks into my stay, I began to understand that I'd been suffering from a deep spiritual malady that I was powerless to cure. That shred of understanding was enough to make me pay attention when AA member Tom C. paid me a visit and urged me to begin Step Eleven on that fateful day.

After rehab, Tom became my close friend and later my sponsor, and I was eager to follow his direction. I would wake up each morning and meditate for thirty minutes, as instructed. Then I would shower, dress, and get myself to meetings or therapy sessions.

A few members of my home group told me meditating was a bad idea for someone so new to recovery. They urged me to take the Steps in order, suggesting I tackle the Eleventh Step only after I had more sobriety under my belt. But my sponsor said to continue my practice, explaining that daily prayer and meditation would help me "truly understand that recovery is the result of a spiritual disconnect."

So I sat.

Let me tell you, sitting still in meditation can be a challenge for the healthiest of human beings, but for someone like me, someone newly clean and sober, it was a climb up Mount Everest. Every time I hit the cushion, my mind would churn with fear, resentment, and anxiety. There were days I just didn't want to be there.

Ironically, what worked in my favor was the tireless work ethic my father had drummed into me all my life. It was an ethic I had come to resent; now, it was a gift that made me driven and determined to attain the peace I'd been promised.

My Path to Sanity

I prayed, meditated, and sat, and sat, and sat, struggling against an onslaught of feelings. After a few weeks, I finally glimpsed the serenity I'd been told about. But I was far from convinced that the emotional pain it took to get there was worth it.

Natalie Goldberg, an author and Zen Buddhist, describes the feelings that arise during meditation as "great tornadoes of anger and resistance, thunderstorms of joy and grief." With the help of my new mentor, Tom C., and my therapist, I faced the tornadoes and thunderstorms of feeling, released them, and moved on.

After only a few months, the sense of serenity I felt was indescribable. I could hear myself breathe! I learned how to focus on my breath, and when my mind wandered, I would turn my attention to the next inhalation, over and over again, no matter how many times I was distracted.

At first, I treated myself with the same impatience and criticism that had been my lifelong pattern. But as the months went by, I understood that this was just the nature of the mind and I was able to direct my attention back to my breath, lovingly and without judgment. When I finally found my way to the other side, I discovered a sense of peace and deep understanding that I had never experienced before.

After that, it was clear that prayer and meditation were the keys to my sanity. Not only had I found relief from drug and alcohol cravings, but more importantly, from the emotional turmoil that had consumed me. All I had to do was sit still, close my eyes, and breathe to experience the part of me that is pure and eternal, the part that was never addicted to drugs or alcohol and never could be. I prayed for guidance from that part of myself and soon I heard answers in the form of insight, knowledge, intuition, and a very clear, unwavering sense of purpose.

My Seven Years of Meditation and Study

This newfound direction led me on what became a seven-year journey of meditation and study with some of the planet's great healers and spiritual teachers. My thirst for knowledge took me to retreat centers and conferences where I met like-minded seekers who became my friends, colleagues, and teachers.

I tore through every book on spirituality I could find, seeking out and studying with some of the masters whose works I'd been reading. These included Buddhist monk, teacher, and Nobel Peace Prize–nominee Thich Nhat Hanh; bestselling author and mind-body medicine pioneer Deepak Chopra, M.D.; and Jon Kabat-Zinn, Ph.D., founder of the groundbreaking Stress-Reduction Clinic and Center for Mindfulness in Medicine, Health Care, and Society at the University of Massachusetts Medical School.

Under their instruction, I earned certifications as a meditation teacher. I went on to study with Yogi Amrit Desai and became a certified yoga instructor. On my new path, I found myself invited to help bring His Holiness the Dalai Lama to Washington, D.C. I was astonished when I found myself in a position to receive his private blessing.

Among the other pioneers I met was Andrew Weil, M.D., the renowned physician and bestselling author who spearheaded the integrative medicine movement in this country. I was fascinated by his philosophy that Western and alternative medicine could be used effectively in combination with nutrition, exercise, stress reduction, and the body's natural ability to heal.

A Passion for Healing

Inspired by Weil's work, I was determined to move healthcare toward a new model, one that emphasized that it is more important to know what kind of person has a disease than what kind of disease a person has. In pursuit of that vision, I invited healers in my community to join me in opening the Inner Harmony Wellness Center in Scranton in 1997.

The center, now with a second branch on the island of St. Maarten, offers traditional medicine as well as acupuncture, massage, psychotherapy, meditation, and many other alternative forms of healing. It took many years for the center to turn a profit, but for the first time in my life, I didn't care about money. This was a labor of love.

Today, the Inner Harmony Wellness Center sets standards for alternative health facilities around the country. Appreciating the importance of our vision, Andrew Weil invited me several years back to serve a term as chairman of the board of the National Integrative Medicine Council, formed to influence and guide the future of both holistic and mainstream healthcare.

Weil further opened my eyes to the possibilities of healing when he invited me to join him and a group of his friends and colleagues on a three-week tour of Africa to study indigenous healing, ritual, and ceremony. Together, we toured South Africa, Zimbabwe, Namibia, and Botswana, stopping in villages where denizens hunt for their food with sticks and spears. Weil, botany expert and scholar of the healing properties of plants, herbs, and wildlife, had organized the trip to study the healing practices of shamans and medicine men of ancient cultures.

In each village, often with the help of translators, we learned about the local flora and fauna. The Kalahari Bushmen, one of the oldest hunter-gatherer tribes on earth, fascinated me. They had a remarkable relationship with nature. They would walk us through the woods, explaining how they wasted nothing, including the skin, bones, and feathers of the animals they hunted.

The tribe's healers treated the land as if it were their corner drugstore. They knew which twig to snap, from what tree to grab a leaf for a healing tea, what bone to suck, and what bug to eat. They harvested ants for their medicinal properties.

We observed the tribe's healing techniques, practiced from a place of deep spiritual connection, and watched in awe as they called upon spirit guides through ritual, ceremony, dance, sacrifice, and worship. They practiced hands-on healing, moving into deep trances to connect with unseen energies. Time stood still in their presence.

It was the turn of the twenty-first century, yet here was a culture still steeped in magic, ritual, and myth. The amazing thing was—and what excited all of us, especially Andrew Weil—was that the medicines of the Kalahari and the other indigenous tribes we encountered *worked*.

A Deeper Sense of Spirituality

My travels continued, and a year after this trip, I joined Joan Borysenko for a group tour of India. Joan, an author and expert in the field of psychoneuroimmunology (also known as the mind-body connection), outlined an ambitious itinerary that included Buddhist, Hindu, Jewish, Islamic, Sikh, Jain, and Christian sites. We visited ashrams built by some of India's most renowned spiritual leaders.

In the city of Puttaparthi, during a visit to Sri Sathya Sai Baba's ashram, I participated in a ceremony that transported me to a level of consciousness higher than any I had ever known. Our group had joined thousands of worshippers at the temple before sunrise to recite the famous *Gayatri Mantra,* an ancient Hindu prayer often called the "mantra of all mantras." It is a solemn prayer that is a plea for wisdom.

The sound and vibration of so many people chanting this beautiful mantra together for hours and hours overtook me. I dropped into a state of meditation so deep I could no longer tell whether I was chanting aloud or not. I had *become* the mantra.

When it stopped very suddenly, I heard an amazing silence, a soundless peace that resonated to my core.

When the ashram's founder, Sai Baba, finally arrived in the temple, I understood that the powerful energy I had been feeling since I had stepped on the grounds emanated from this teacher's deep spiritual connection to the energies of the universe. He seemed to exist on another plane, to glow from within as he greeted the crowd.

The energy of the day and that man inspired me to return to India again to visit more ashrams, including those run by Sri Sri Ravi Shankar, Sri Aurobindo, Mata Amritanandamayi, and Ramana Maharshi. Each time I returned home from India I was forever changed. I understood from these trips—on a cellular level—that we are a miraculous collection of energy, and that life is to be led as a prayer with devotion to the unknown forces that create us and move through us.

Out of the Cave

At the end of those amazing seven years, a few AA friends approached me in something of a spiritual intervention. They urged me to "come out of my cave," to leave the insulated existence I had been living and give back to my community and the world.

I knew they were right. I had opened the Inner Harmony Wellness Centers, but had taken a hands-off approach, letting administrators handle day-to-day operations. I knew it was time to get involved with the center again and to begin teaching.

As I moved slowly back into society, people who heard my story, who knew about the deep work I had done, sought my help in spiritual matters, particularly people in Twelve Step programs who were looking to deepen their connection to a higher power through the Eleventh Step. I taught workshops ranging in length from one afternoon to month-long intensives. My seminars included exercises in self-examination, spiritual discourse, and instruction in prayer and meditation in many forms—sitting, yoga, walking, mantra, and breath work. It became clear that helping people find a sense of peace and purpose was giving my own life new meaning.

I continued my work at the Wellness Center, but I also returned to school to earn a degree in transpersonal psychology, allowing me to become a professional counselor. I wanted to help anyone who asked for guidance. And I did. These included people in my community, in rehabilitation centers, in prisons, and in schools—anywhere I was called.

More recently, I cofounded the Integrative Life Center, a cutting-edge outpatient addiction facility in Nashville. Next, I will begin my doctoral studies in mind-body medicine.

My journey through recovery has been an unbelievable ride, one that rivals any drag race record I could ever break. Today, my work is as far removed from transmissions, carburetors, and tires as it gets. Today, my days are dedicated to helping others find physical and spiritual health, to sharing the path to peace and understanding that has so blessed my life.

I often joke that I have no idea how I got here. I have no idea how a car guy who once sold automotive parts for a living came to spend his days praying, meditating, chanting, practicing yoga, teaching, and reading volumes about spirituality, philosophy, and social evolution. I have no idea how a man once obsessed with the cut of his jacket became dedicated to exploring the fabric of his soul and to being an agent of positive change in the world.

Never in my wildest dreams could I have imagined that I would meditate in ancient temples, study with yogis, chant with prison inmates, or teach school children how to pay attention to their breath. I had no idea I would dedicate my life to healing and helping others. I look back on this unfathomable journey and smile knowing that the same district attorney who once gave me an ultimatum fifteen years ago is now a friend and personal cheerleader. He is also now a judge who invited me to teach a county-sponsored program for people struggling with addiction.

How did I get here? Such are the gifts of prayer and meditation. Such are the gifts of turning inward, of quieting the mind, of listening for guidance, and taking the next right step. Such are the gifts of knowing that peace is as close as your next breath.

INNER HARMONY EXERCISE

A Higher Power of Your Understanding

The Second Step states that we "came to believe that a Power greater than ourselves could restore us to sanity." The words "came to believe" imply that by working the Steps, we receive the promises of the program, have a spiritual awakening, and gradually gain an understanding of a higher power that is capable of returning us to a state of sanity. But when you start the Eleventh Step *before* you have this awakening, to whom or what are you praying, and from whom or what are you asking for guidance?

If you already practice a particular religion and/or have a clear sense of God or higher power, feel free to use this exercise to expand on that understanding. However, if the concept of a higher power seems foreign, abstract, or even distasteful, this exercise will help you explore ideas of a higher power you might find compelling.

What you need: A journal, a pen, a timer.

What to do:

1. Close your eyes and take a deep breath. Think about something that inspires your awe. Is it the power of nature—a magnificent vista or the night sky? Or is it science? Love? Perhaps it's beautiful music. Art. Intellect. Philosophy. Notice how this sense of awe feels in your body. Do you experience warmth in your chest? Do you relax more? Set the timer for five minutes and without stopping write down any feelings or insights that come up.

2. Close your eyes again and think about someone you love and trust. Maybe it's a sponsor, a friend, relative, teacher, or child. Or maybe it's a great leader or scholar you don't know personally. Take time to think about the qualities this person has. What makes him or her lovable and trustworthy? Set the timer for five minutes and without stopping, write down the qualities that come to mind. Does this person embody patience, kindness, and compassion? Does he or she have a great sense of humor? What about this person makes your heart feel open and allows you to feel safe?

3. Close your eyes again. If you attend meetings, bring to mind a speaker or fellow member whom you have seen make positive changes. Or think of someone else you know who has changed for the better. It could be a person who has remained sober or abstinent for a long time; someone who battled the odds to land a new job; or someone who resolved a difficult relationship issue. Pick someone who made an impression on you. Set the timer for five minutes, and without stopping, write about this person. Has witnessing his growth encouraged you, made you feel stronger, more hopeful? Does she talk about relying on a higher power? If so, do you draw strength and trust knowing her connection with a higher power made a difference? Write down any thoughts or feelings this brings up.

4. Read what you have written. See if you can identify qualities or characteristics that you would want in a higher power. As you go about your day, find a few times to breathe and reflect on the feelings, thoughts, and concepts this exercise inspires. Try to recall these ideas when you feel confused, stressed, or at a loss for what to do next. Let go of solving your problems, even if only for a few minutes, and simply spend

time pondering what you have written. Do you feel even the smallest sense of relief? Does your situation improve even slightly? Practice relying on the power of these feelings as a source of strength and encouragement throughout your day.

Finding a higher power of your understanding is a process that requires participation, practice, conscious effort, and noticing what works and when. Use your journal to note how turning to a higher power (even a vague idea of one) shifts and changes your experience in the moment and beyond.

You will see Inner Harmony exercises at the end of each chapter. Many of these exercises ask you to write down thoughts, feelings, memories, and so forth. You might find it helpful to keep a journal so you can keep your work in one place and refer back to it as needed. I also suggest using this journal to write down prayers and record any insights that arise while you read this book or after you complete a meditation. As time goes on, it can be helpful to go back and reread what you wrote, taking stock of shifts in your attitudes and changes in the circumstances of your life.

2

WHAT IS PRAYER?
WHAT IS MEDITATION?

*We embark upon the creation of a
peaceful lifestyle by recognizing the need, daily,
to cleanse our minds, just as we cleanse our bodies.
Through morning prayers and meditation, we embark
upon the day spiritually prepared.*

—Marianne Williamson

WHETHER YOU ARE CHRISTIAN, Muslim, Jewish, Buddhist, Hindu, Sikh, agnostic, or even the most skeptical atheist, you have experienced awe. You have stood on the shores of a mighty ocean, bathed in the light of a blazing sunset, or marveled at the miracle of birth and known that the universe is bigger than you are. You have also been awed by the destructive power of the universe—the devastation of an earthquake or the ravages of disease stealing life from a loved one.

Perhaps you consider such events acts of God, Spirit, or the forces of nature, but as human beings we all know, without a doubt, that there is a force—a higher power—that is far beyond our understanding. The Eleventh Step suggests that we seek "through prayer and meditation to improve our conscious contact" with this power, however we envision It, Him, or Her—and that we do this for two reasons only:

1. To gain knowledge of a higher power's will for us.
2. To find strength to act on this guidance.

Acting As If

Of course, it might be a huge leap for you to go from acknowledging the existence of a higher power to believing it has a "will" for you and that it can be "contacted" for guidance. The truth is, you don't have to believe it any more than you have to believe that embarking on a program of physical fitness will make you feel better, have more energy, and lose weight. You just have to begin. I suggest that you act "as if" a higher power has a will for you and that making conscious contact with it will make a difference. You don't have to believe it. You just have to try it. Give prayer and meditation a chance for a month and see if anything shifts. Yes, this is an act of faith, and if you are an atheist or agnostic, that might be a hard pill to swallow. But don't you exercise as an act of faith because you know it has worked for other people in the past? So, too, have people in recovery relied on prayer and meditation and made incredible advances in their lives. Fortunately, prayer and meditation are free, so you have absolutely nothing to lose by trying it for thirty days. At the end of a month, evaluate your progress and see if you want to continue.

Surrender

When we embark on a path of recovery—whether we seek change through the Twelve Steps or not—we learn that we have to surrender our old ways of thinking and acting or we will lapse back into our addiction and the life of misery it brought us. There is a popular saying among people in recovery: "Your best thinking got you here." So, how do you change your "best thinking"? How do you move beyond the limitations of your own mind?

Prayer and meditation are the tools that help you do this. *When you pray, you talk to your higher power, and when you meditate, you listen for and experience any guidance you receive.* We will talk more about the mechanics of prayer and meditation in Chapters 5 and 9, but for now let's examine the role these practices play in your recovery and your life.

Prayer

Prayer likely found its way into the human experience when basic needs went unmet. Perhaps drought destroyed vegetation, killing off livestock and leading to famine. Or hurricanes, tornadoes, or floods wiped out a community. Despair and hopelessness followed. When personal resources are exhausted, when all seems lost, it is human nature to look to the heavens for help.

As we evolved, people prayed for more complex reasons: for personal benefit, to assist others, for worship, to give thanks, and to seek forgiveness, among other things. The Eleventh Step, however, is quite clear in its directive that we pray *only* for guidance and strength. Not for things we want or think we or other people need. Not for new cars or the perfect mate, or—noble as it may seem—for other people's success.

We *do* pray that our thinking and actions be directed from a higher place, that Spirit, God, Divinity, the Force, whatever we call our higher power, guides our thoughts and actions. Instead of praying for specific things or outcomes, we ask: What should I do in any given situation? How should I act? Where should I go? So, if you want to find a meaningful career, if you are seeking the perfect mate, or you want to support a friend, you might ask: Give me guidance about a new job. What should I look for in a mate? How can I help a loved one find their way?

Why does the Eleventh Step suggest we pray this way? Because we are in recovery from addiction. If we had a clear idea what was good for others and ourselves, would we spend our time in meeting halls, unraveling the wreckage of our lives, searching for relief from the insanity that has plagued us? Remember: our best thinking got us here.

I am being droll, but the truth is, if you want to move toward sanity you no longer have the luxury of relying solely on your own guidance. In some ways, you knew this the day you reached out for help with your addiction—by picking up this book, going to a meeting, or seeing a therapist. You sought help from someone or something outside yourself.

Many religious traditions specify rituals for prayer: Catholicism asks followers to pray in the kneeling position with hands clasped; the Jewish tradition wants worshippers to wear a *talit,* a fringed shawl, when praying; Muslims pray five times a day facing toward Mecca.

There are as many ways to pray as there are people. Some pray during a walk in the woods, others sing their prayers, and some consider scientific inquiry its own form of prayer. For our purposes, it makes no difference how your prayer *looks,* it only matters that your *intention* is to ask for guidance and strength from a higher power of your understanding.

Meditation

What is meditation? When we meditate we consciously focus our attention on *one* thing. This can be a sensation, thought, sound, an image, idea, or activity. But our purpose in striving for this one-pointed focus is to quiet the mind.

Try it. Close your eyes and take a long, deep breath. Focus on the sounds outside for fifteen seconds. . . .

What did you hear? A truck passing? A dog barking? The wind? How do you feel? A little calmer, quieter? You just meditated. You *intentionally* shifted your focus from the book you are reading to the sounds outside.

The ability to shift your attention is the result of millions of cells, synapses, neurons, and chemicals working together. It is at once a miracle and no big deal. You do it all the time. It's just that when you are meditating, you intentionally shift your focus for periods that can last anywhere from a few seconds to a few hours, and in the case of some Buddhist monks months at a time.

Throughout the ages, people have turned to meditation for myriad reasons. Most religions encourage quieting the mind to contemplate God. Some meditation practices promise a path to nirvana, or total enlightenment. Martial artists use meditation to achieve the mental focus needed for competitions.

Most people are familiar with sitting meditation, the practice in which one assumes the lotus position with legs crossed, or settles into a chair and focuses on the breath or other bodily sensations. This kind of meditation can also be practiced by chanting a mantra (a specific word or sound), audibly or internally, with the focus being music or vibration.

Yoga and walking meditation use the breath and movement as a point of focus. Meditation can also involve fingering or counting beads (japa mala or rosary), active manipulation of the breath (called *pranayama* in yoga practice), staring at a lit candle, or even drawing. Any of these practices can be done alone or in groups, but the common thread is one-pointed focus.

We practice meditation to quiet the mind so we can listen for guidance, renew our spirit, and gain the emotional, spiritual, and physical strength we need to act on the information we receive—that is, to act differently than we have in the past.

This does not mean we don't enjoy other benefits of meditation, including reduced anxiety, improved health, mental clarity, energy, and serenity. But the intention we set when we meditate as part of the Eleventh Step is to listen for guidance and receive strength so we might move toward our highest self.

By the way, when I use the term *listen,* I don't suggest a booming voice will speak to you or that you will hear whispers from angels (though both have been known to happen). Guidance can come in any form: as a thought, a feeling, a sense, or intuition. Guidance can show up hours, days, weeks, months, or even years after you meditate. It can come from a person, a book, a film, a song, or as an "aha! moment" that strikes while you're doing dishes.

When we meditate, we become fine-tuned receivers clear of cluttered thinking. The more we meditate, the deeper we go, and the more we experience states of profound clarity, stillness, and insight.

Deepening Conscious Contact

Notice that the Eleventh Step suggests that we seek to *improve* our conscious contact with a higher power. This implies that, at some point, we have already made such contact, either through the awe we spoke of earlier, a religious epiphany, by practicing the first three Steps, or through some other spiritual experience. Our recovery depends on our willingness to deepen this connection— however strong or tenous—to renew our spirit on an ongoing basis.

This is where commitment and discipline come in—terrifying words for those of us who have struggled with addiction. Most of us, myself included, functioned on self-will, running for the hills when anything smacked of obligation. But just as some of us have committed to our recovery one day at a time by attending meetings, working the Steps, calling our sponsors, or whatever path we have chosen, we can also commit to the practice of prayer and meditation one day at a time.

On our new path, we renounce old patterns and old ways of living. We agree to become rigorously honest, dedicating ourselves to helping others and giving up our old ways of doing things. But old habits do die hard. That is why we need to check in with our higher power regularly. If we are not vigilant about connecting with our Source, it is easy to let the physical world pull us back, to lose sight of our purpose and direction.

You do not have to practice prayer and meditation as if you were a monk, but it is a good idea to find some time in your day to pray and meditate, to get quiet, and to remind yourself and the universe that you are willing to change. Create a schedule of practice that works for you. Your practice can begin with as little as one minute.

As you will see, praying and meditating require that you be compassionate and patient with yourself. Give yourself permission to be where you are. If you can do this, you will want to go deeper into your practice. You will welcome prayer and mediation as anchors in your day.

But if you badger yourself, your practice will be a chore, and you will not want to continue. Move forward gradually, in small, manageable increments, and you will begin to receive the guidance you are seeking. It will come through with more frequency and clarity; prayer and meditation will become a beautiful part of your life.

Roadblocks to Prayer and Meditation

Many people in Twelve Step programs—even the best intentioned—struggle to pray and meditate on a regular basis. As I have said, students come to me exasperated because they cannot find a way to incorporate prayer and meditation into their daily lives. Below are a few of the most common concerns I hear, along with suggestions for overcoming them. Later, in Chapter 12, we'll explore some pitfalls that often occur on your spiritual journey *after* you've had more experience with the Eleventh Step. But for now, let's look at some issues that can make anyone resistant to regular prayer and meditation.

I Don't Have Time

This is the concern I hear most frequently. Work, relationships, children, sick parents—life's endless string of to-dos—can be overwhelming. Add meetings, service, and therapy into the mix, and regular prayer and meditation can seem like one more obligation.

RECOMMENDATION: If you can make a habit of washing your face and brushing your teeth each morning and night, you can make a habit of praying and meditating each day. For those of you with a lot of resistance, begin with one minute of prayer and meditation in the morning and one minute at night.

You might balk at this suggestion. "Are you kidding? What good will that do?" But if you can let go of all-or-nothing thinking and begin a daily practice, dedicating just a small amount of time to prayer and meditation, you will quickly find that you *want* to add another minute, then even another five minutes. Not only that, you will start to feel as if you have more time in your day—your thinking gets clearer, you become more organized, and you start to use your time more efficiently.

If you need motivation to pray and meditate for even a minute, just think how easy it is to waste a minute watching television, reading e-mails, texting, or flipping through a magazine. Do you really want to let time slip away on something frivolous, or would you rather use it to move forward in your recovery? One minute.

The goal is to create a routine, to make prayer and meditation a new habit, even if that habit lasts for only a couple of minutes a day. It's pretty hard to get frustrated after a couple of minutes. From there, you might find that you want to make more time for your practice, lengthen it, and even switch up the form of meditation you use. When you're ready, you can turn to Chapter 10 and find meditation sessions lasting from one minute to two hours. Try increasing the sessions in five- or fifteen-minute increments as your schedule allows. You will discover that it gets easier to sit for longer periods, and you will *want* to carve out more time. Ideally, you will work your way up to thirty minutes a day. However, if it is a choice between meditating for one minute or not at all, just do what you can.

I Can't Find a Quiet Place

People complain that they have no space to themselves, no room in their home or workplace where they can do their Eleventh Step work undisturbed. Children, spouses, bosses, and even pets barge in on them with never-ending needs that drain their time and energy. Boundaries are broken over and over again.

Recommendation: Wake up a half hour before everyone in your home or go to sleep a half hour later. Buy a timer. Find a quiet room, corner, or patio, and let the people in your life know that they can talk to you *after* the timer goes off. This sets a clear boundary and lets you feel secure that you will not be interrupted for a specific amount of time.

Alternatively, many houses of worship keep their sanctuaries open to the public for some portion of the day. If your religious institution is far away, or even if you are not religious at all, there is no rule that says you can't pray and meditate in someone else's house of worship, unless you find this personally objectionable. Few people will check your religious credentials at the door or ask to which God you are praying.

Additionally, most cities and towns have a city hall, library, or community center where there are empty rooms in which to sit quietly for at least a few minutes. If the weather is nice, a quiet park or a bench will do. When all else fails, you can pray and meditate in your parked car or in the bathroom. All you need is a few minutes or more of uninterrupted time.

If you feel self-conscious praying and meditating in a public place, wear headphones. You can listen to a guided mediation, recorded chants, or soothing music. (See the Suggested Reading and Listening section at the back of this book). If you prefer silence, you can always wear earphones—but you don't have to connect them. No one looks twice if they think you are listening to music with your eyes closed.

I Just Can't Sit Still

Many people in recovery, especially those in the early stages, just cannot sit still. Their legs twitch, their backs and legs get stiff, or they can't get comfortable.

RECOMMENDATION: If physical symptoms prevent you from practicing sitting meditation, try yoga or walking meditation (see Chapter 9). These are great alternatives to more static practices. They are active, good for your health, and effective at quieting the mind. If you are determined to practice sitting meditation, try alternating between sitting and standing, or sitting and yoga, but strive to keep your focus as you transition from one practice to the other.

There is also no law that says you have to meditate sitting on the ground with your legs in the lotus position (crossed). If it helps you to remain still, you can use a chair, sit against a wall with your legs in front of you, or even sit with one leg tucked in and the other straight out. It is only important that your spine is straight so energy flows through your body unimpeded.

My Mind Races

Almost everyone struggles with this issue. You try to quiet your mind, but intrusive to-do lists take over, or your inner critic harangues you about wasting time. Or you think you're praying and meditating *all wrong*. For some of us, getting quiet stirs up a flood of emotion that addiction has kept at bay, sometimes for decades. Anger, regret, fear, anxiety, guilt, and shame overwhelm us. Who wants to sit still through that?

RECOMMENDATION: Meditation is also called *mindfulness*. When we meditate, we foster awareness. We pay attention to where our mind is. If we notice that our mind has wandered, we note what we are thinking and then move our attention back to our point of focus. If you simply cannot keep your to-do list at bay, keep a pad and pen nearby to jot down tasks . . . then forget about them and return to your practice. They will be there in a few minutes or half an hour.

If emotions keep you from staying focused, again, simply notice them and feel them. If they are not overwhelming, gently guide your mind back to the breath or other point of focus. If you start to cry, let it happen. Love yourself through the tears. You will not cry forever.

See the feelings through, and when you are done, gently guide your focus back to the breath, sound, posture, or whatever you have chosen as your point of focus. The more you pray and meditate, the easier it gets to let feelings pass through you. It is vital that you cultivate patience, compassion, and a sense of acceptance.

The ability to return your attention to one point is not just a wonderful tool for quieting the mind during meditation, it is a resource you can draw upon at any point during your day. When people, places, or things test your patience, you can recall how you shifted your attention during meditation. Use this skill to focus on more positive aspects of a challenging situation; for example, you can focus on any lessons a situation might offer rather than annoyances that might arise.

That said, even the most experienced spiritual practitioners have days when they simply cannot focus. What sets them apart is that they accept these distractions as part of their practice. They notice that they can't focus, they accept it, and continue to meditate. Sometimes, your entire meditation session will be spent worrying, thinking, or even obsessing. That's okay. If you only pay attention to one breath, one sensation, your practice has been successful. If you sat through the whole thing and thought, *Wow, my mind won't shut off,* you have fostered some awareness. This is meditation. The next session will be different, probably not perfect, but different.

If you simply cannot turn off your mind, read Chapter 9 to learn about yoga, chanting, and mantras such as "Om" or "Yam." Moving and sound meditations are excellent choices when your thoughts won't quiet down. When you chant a mantra, for example, the mind becomes focused more easily because it cannot hold two thoughts simultaneously.

Pranayama, especially *Ujjayi* breathing (a diaphragmatic, rasping breath), is another more active form of meditation that engages the body and senses more fully Finally, if you feel completely powerless over racing thoughts and feelings, *pray* for guidance to get through the process.

I Have Trouble with the Idea of God and a Higher Power

When I first walked into AA, I was told to surrender. I had a hard time with this suggestion. I was *willing* to surrender, but had no idea how to do it. Surrender to whom? To what? I wasn't raised with much religious training. Was I supposed to surrender to an old man on a throne? To a tree? To the stars?

I know I am not alone. Many people struggle with "the God question." For some, the concept of a higher power seems too vague and amorphous. Others don't believe in any kind of God, or at least not one that hears their individual prayers. There are those who have the opposite problem. Their concept of a higher power is very specific: punishing, judgmental, and negative.

RECOMMENDATION: Refer to the Inner Harmony exercise at the end of Chapter 1 to help you explore concepts of a higher power that resonate for you. This exercise can also help you build on any idea of a higher power that you already have.

But there is another way to think about a higher power—*experientially*. When you meditate, you experience a deep mental state; you feel a powerful shift in your body and mind. This in itself is a concrete experience of a higher power.

When I first began my meditation practice, I found it extremely helpful to pray and meditate to this internal experience. I asked that this experience of peace and stillness help me find answers and guidance. Over time, by deepening my connection with this experience, I began to see results in my life; and I came to rely on the interplay between prayer, meditation, and this experience. I did not need a mental image of a higher power or even a name or label. I simply witnessed the difference that emerged in the way I reacted and thought. This became my higher power. The quality and depth of my relationships with others changed dramatically. I felt a sense of love, compassion, and direction.

Praying to and believing in a higher power can be a bit of a chicken and egg situation. You start by being *willing* to connect with a higher power, even if that idea is vague and incomplete. But when this willingness yields perceptible internal and external shifts, you start to understand the nature of this interchange. A feeling and rhythm develops. You ask your higher power for guidance, you get answers and understanding, and the feelings and sense of release you get from relying on a higher power encourage you to return to this source for guidance again.

As an analogy, think about the game of tennis. You hit a ball over the net and the other person hits it back. If you are a beginner, it can be an awkward dance: you might miss the ball, lob it into the air, smash it into the net. You are thinking about technique and form. But through repeated practice the technique becomes set in your body and mind. You find a rhythm, you discover the "sweet spot" on the racket, and you figure out when and how hard to hit the ball. You don't have to analyze how or why this happens. As human beings we know that we are a complex network of muscles, tissue, and mental wiring, and that practice and repetition build mental and physical dexterity. Soon, you start paying attention to your opponent rather than yourself. You focus on playing the game.

Prayer and meditation are no different. If you take steps to establish a spiritual connection through prayer and meditation, if you work toward mastering these practices, you begin to feel the presence and rhythm of a higher power in your life.

A Life of Prayer and Meditation

Over the years, I have known states of consciousness so profoundly peaceful and beautiful that I did not want to come out of them. I have felt so attuned to the world around me that I could feel subtle energies flowing through and past my body. I have experienced what it is like to move beyond thought to a state in which I understood that a higher power is inside me at all times. I don't pretend to live in that state every minute of the day, but it has become easier for me to return there whenever I need to, to find peace in my next breath.

This state is attainable. Gurus, shamans, priests, rabbis, saints, prophets, and spiritual teachers throughout history have given accounts of this feeling of connectedness. While you do not have to be a monk or a holy person to experience this sense of union, it does require making a small beginning. Once you do, you begin to enjoy a clarity of mind and a sense of direction that makes you want to establish a regular spiritual practice. If you choose to delve deeper, you can create miniretreats on your own or with other meditators. There are also meditation centers (see the Resources section at the back of this book) that provide extended retreats where you can learn even more about these deeper states of consciousness. But no amount of talking or writing can convey the experience. You have to walk the walk and live it for yourself.

INNER HARMONY EXERCISE

A Prayer for Today and Tomorrow

The Eleventh Step suggests we pray *only* for knowledge of our higher power's will for us and the power to carry it out. Does this mean you cannot ask your higher power to help you with something specific? Of course you can. But there is a way to phrase your prayer so you are not predetermining the answer you want to hear. The idea is to remain open to possibility.

What you need: A timer, a pen, your journal, and a calendar.

What to do: Take a deep breath and mentally scan your body for tension. Are your shoulders tense? Is your brow furrowed? Does your chest feel heavy? Breathe in and let the exhalation help you let go of tension and holding. Breathe again.

Now, bring to mind a pressing issue. Some examples: My son is having trouble in school; the mortgage is overdue; I want to get married; my wife wants a divorce.

Write down your issue, doing your best to stay relaxed even while thinking about something difficult. Take another deep breath, and formulate a prayer about this issue, trying not to ask for specific results. For example: What would you have me do (or not do) about my son's troubles in school and in life? What is your will about my finances and living situation? Is this the best time to pursue a romantic relationship? Please show me how to create a loving, healthy relationship with my spouse.

One more deep breath. Now, without stopping or thinking too much, spend ten minutes writing anything that comes to you. If nothing occurs to you, that's fine, too. The only rule is to keep your pen moving. Don't stop. Even if you write "absolutely nothing is coming to me and it's making me really mad," it doesn't matter. Don't judge, filter, or read what you've written. Just keep going until the time is up. Do not reread what you've written.

Take a deep breath and thank your higher power for any guidance you've received today or that you might receive in the future. Reaffirm that you are open and willing to receive guidance from within, from other people, from books, newspapers, anywhere.

The next day, reread what you have written. Notice what, if anything, has shifted. Then write a reminder in your datebook or calendar to reread what you've written two weeks from now. Take note of any changes. You can repeat this process in six months or a year. It is a powerful way to mark the progress of your spiritual growth.

3

THE INNER HARMONY
APPROACH

Simple witnessing awareness . . . is Spirit itself,
is the enlightened mind itself, is the Buddha-nature
itself, is God itself, in its entirety.

—Ken Wilber

W E BUSY OURSELVES WITH DAILY CONCERNS.
We wake up to blaring alarm clocks, fight traffic, go to
work, put food on the table, raise kids, rush in and out of stores,
schedule doctor appointments, go on vacations, cry, laugh, sing,
play, and sleep—the hubbub of life. We do these things as our tiny
blue planet spins quietly on its axis, orbiting an unimpressive star
on an outer band of the Milky Way—itself an unremarkable gal-
axy that spirals through a universe more immense than we can
possibly comprehend.

If we're lucky, we spend seventy-five to a hundred years inhaling oxygen and exhaling carbon dioxide on this wild spinning ride, our bodies regenerating with the help of protein, carbohydrates, minerals, and other nutrients our planet yields—all of it the stuff of exploding stars.

We might reproduce, and then, like generations before us, our flesh and bones return to the earth and we fade into history. As Joni Mitchell put it in her classic song "Woodstock" . . . *we are stardust.*

Most days we forget this simple truth. Most days we forget just how amazing yet impermanent our existence is, what a miracle it is that we *are*. Instead, we fret, obsess, panic, control, plot, and wrestle with life. We fight with ourselves and with each other. We long for more than we have no matter how much we've got. Societies wage wars, befriend enemies, then find new wars to fight, and it starts over again.

So what is important? What is real?

The great American author Mark Twain once said, "I am an old man and have known a great many troubles, but most of them never happened." Twain knew that so many of the woes we believe are real, aren't.

But some things remain true. Unless we suffer from severe mental illness, disease, or brain injury, we as human beings share a basic desire: We long for our time on earth to be physically comfortable and spiritually and emotionally fulfilling. After our physical needs are met, we want our lives to *mean* something.

We yearn to express our unique gifts, strengths, visions, and concerns in ways that feel right, that have a positive impact on our family, friends, community, and planet. We want to leave the world better for our having been here. Some people are more conscious of this desire than others, but dig deep enough into anyone's psyche, and the need to feel connected to each other and to a higher purpose is a common thread.

Most of us know at least one person who leads a fulfilling life, who has a clear sense of purpose and connection. This friend, relative, or acquaintance certainly experiences sadness and stress, but for the most part, he or she seems to wake up happy to be alive and joyous about what the day will bring.

Some people come to this state naturally, some arrive at it through a spiritual awakening, and others work to achieve it, but for whatever reason, their lives flow with ease; they are connected to God, Christ, Yahweh, Buddha nature, a higher power, whatever you want to call it. Their soul is connected to spirit.

Soul, Spirit, and Ego

People often use the words *soul* and *spirit* interchangeably. But I consider the soul the part of us that witnesses existence, that watches, that *is*. The soul is aware of thoughts and feelings coming and going. It is quiet, peaceful, and alert. The soul is silent.

Spirit, on the other hand, is larger than we are. It is our higher power, God, the unifying forces of the universe. It animates our bodies, creates babies, makes gardens grow. It is the force behind exploding atoms; it creates organization and chaos. Our souls are connected to spirit the same way waves are connected to the ocean. They are not separate, yet each wave is distinguishable, unique. Similarly, each of our souls is a beautiful, one-of-a kind expression of the spirit that created it.

The *ego* is the part of us that thinks, examines, analyzes, and judges. It makes lists, gets you places on time, tells you to work hard. The ego is essential to your survival. It keeps you comfortable and educated. The ego pushes us forward as a species. It has brought humankind out of caves and into the modern era.

The ego is good at survival because it keeps you alert. It constantly compares you to other people and tells you you're not enough; it worries, frets, and fusses. In its never-ending quest to keep you comfortable and alive the ego convinces you that you're in danger. It tells you we are all separate from one another, that we are enemies. The material realm is all that matters to the ego, so it fills you with fear that everything can be taken away if you don't constantly look over your shoulder.

Most of us no longer survive in the wild, and, in industrialized nations, our basic needs are usually met. But our egos, hardwired into our brains, have not caught up with this fact. The ego is not a bad thing, but it looks out for itself and its own concerns. In that regard, the ego is not terribly fond of your soul or of spirit because it knows, on some level, that spirit is so powerful, so glorious, that if you ever really experienced it, *knew it,* you might not tend to the tasks of daily living.

Therefore, the ego does its best to distract you from your soul and spirit. And, as is often the case for addictive personalities, the ego often goes too far, completely blocking a person's view of his or her soul and spirit. In a sad irony, the ego's noble efforts to protect you often backfire—a soul completely disconnected from spirit no longer wants to cherish the life the ego works so hard to protect.

In the book *My Stroke of Insight: A Brain Scientist's Personal Journey,* author Jill Bolte Taylor recalled what could be described as an epic battle raging between her ego and soul as a stroke consumed her brain. She talked about this experience on the website TED.com, explaining that she felt energies outside the physical plane (spirit) that were so clear and irresistible, so unfettered by rational thinking (ego), that she no longer wanted to remain on earth: "I felt at one with all the energy that was, and it was beautiful there . . . I felt enormous and expansive like a genie liberated from its bottle."

Finally, she mustered whatever mental connectivity she had left, and her soul and ego hammered out a compromise that let her function just long enough to make a lifesaving phone call. The rational part of her mind (ego) reasoned with the part (soul) that longed to reconnect to her source (spirit), that if she could just stay alive she would use her skills as a scientist and stroke survivor to share the incredible insight she had gained:

> I realized: I'm still alive and I have found nirvana. And if I have found nirvana and I am still alive, then everyone who is alive can find nirvana. And I pictured a world full of beautiful, peaceful, compassionate, loving people who knew that they could come to this space at any time and they could purposely choose . . . to find this peace.

Bolte Taylor's "insight" was that when the ego operates in service of the soul, people not only survive but can thrive with their eyes wide open to the amazing power of spirit. This is a beautiful and profound idea.

But most civilized societies operate from a place of ego. Political systems, media, and institutions are usually ego-driven —grounded in materialism, often only paying lip service to the soul's yearning to connect with spirit, or a higher power. Advertising agencies make billions of dollars off of our egos. What sells cosmetics, cars, and exercise equipment better than the idea that we don't have enough and aren't enough?

But human evolution has come to a crossroads. The astonishing scientific and technological advances that have made us so comfortable, that are the ego's gifts, are threatening to destroy us if we cannot balance our egos' needs with those of our souls. If you need proof of what happens when the ego dominates societies, look no further than the collapse of the banking system, the decade-long wars raging around the globe, and the oil gushing into our oceans.

We have stopped valuing our souls' primal need for spirit. Our egos have convinced us that we don't need spirit to thrive. But we are living a lie. We need a connection to spirit as surely as we need food and water. That is why so many of us are crying out in pain, why we turn to drugs and alcohol, food, sex, and so on. We are trying to make the pain stop.

Addiction

Addiction is epidemic. In his book *High Society,* former United States Secretary of Health, Education, and Welfare Joseph Califano Jr. estimated that 100 million people in the United States alone use drugs or stimulants in some form every day—from cigarettes and alcohol to mood-altering prescription drugs and illegal substances.

On a global scale, the United Nations Office on Drugs and Crime reports that about 200 million people misuse drugs, with the estimated cost in lost work, healthcare expenses, and crime running about $180.9 billion for the year 2002 alone. None of these figures account for the toll taken by other forms of addiction such as eating disorders, sex addiction, gambling, and so on.

Clearly, people have lost touch with a sense of purpose and meaning, with a sense that life flows with ease. If you are reading this book then you or someone you know has probably lived a life that does *not* flow. Something went off track. Perhaps a dysfunctional family got in the way of your self-expression, or poverty derailed your happiness, or physical or sexual abuse extinguished your sense of self. Negative teachers and coaches might have eroded your confidence. Chronic pain or illness could have certainly sapped your optimism. Whatever happened, over time, fear took over and the ego dug in with a grip so strong that any connection your soul had to spirit was completely obscured. Life became arduous, difficult, full of pain and suffering.

But each of us remembers what it feels like to be connected to our source, or spirit, even if it was for a fleeting moment, or it is a vague memory from long ago. We know how it feels to be at peace. We know, deep down, that this feeling, this connectedness, is far more real and satisfying than the ego-driven madness we grapple with on a daily basis.

The escape that drugs, alcohol, food, sex, gambling, overspending, undereating, bingeing, workaholism, codependency, and so forth offered us was so enticing because it provided an escape from the ego, a sense of release that mimics the relief we feel when we are connected to a higher power. Addiction offers temporary relief from the onslaught of the ego. But it is just that, *temporary*.

For some of us, just one experience of the relief addiction brought made our yearning for relief spiral out of control. But then, our souls grew even more disconnected from spirit, our egos fought even harder to "protect" us, and the cycle of insanity continued.

Inner Harmony

Somewhere between the madness of the ego and the bliss of the soul's perfect connection to spirit lies balance, equilibrium, a state of inner harmony that comes from understanding the nature of the mind. If you can learn to watch thoughts come and go, to see the ego at work, to thank it, appreciate it, and *choose* whether to buy into it or not, then you can find peace.

If you can remember in any given moment that you are a spiritual being then you can live life unencumbered by drama.

Knowing this truth can save your life, especially if your ego has been slowly killing you, as is usually the case with addiction. Inner harmony comes when you understand that while you abused substances, acted out, or made life a living hell for yourself or others, your soul remained pure, steady, and constant. Spirit—your higher power—was there all along, waiting for your return.

Buddhist monk, meditation master, and author Jack Kornfield writes about rediscovering the soul in his book *After the Ecstasy, the Laundry*:

> We usually take ourselves to be the sum of [our] thoughts, ideas, emotions, and body sensations, but there is nothing solid to them. How can we claim to be our thoughts or opinions or emotions or body when they never stay the same? Perhaps we can take a step back and look at who it is that knows this, the space of knowing in which they arise.

Prayer and meditation are tools that allow you to take this step back, to witness the difference between your soul and ego. Prayer and meditation give you insight into who you are and how your mind works; they allow you to be conscious and spiritually awake.

People have written countless books about their spiritual epiphanies, but it takes practice and commitment to understand this balance for yourself, to be master of your own ego rather than the other way around. It takes willingness to clear away the ego's barrage of thoughts so you can spend time with your soul. Once you do this, you learn to choose which thoughts to believe. You have a say over the quality of your life.

The mind is like a piece of heavy machinery. You can climb aboard and plow down the street without reading the operating instructions, leaving behind a swath of destruction. Or . . . you can master the machine, harness its power, and move mountains.

Which will you do?

Prayer and meditation turbocharge your mind, connect your soul to spirit, make you receptive to ideas, strength, and a sense of purpose that allows you to lead a life filled with compassion and meaning. Understanding this is the gift of sanity that the Twelve Steps promise.

It takes a few concrete, practical tools to stay vigilant, but it is vital that you use them because it is so easy to fall back into old, false beliefs. Many people, places, and things can distract your soul from spirit. But when you learn to focus your attention on one thing—the breath, your body, a mantra—over and over again, you become adept at paying attention to your thoughts. You know how to watch them come and go without hooking into them. Once you master this, once you approach your life with a commitment to inner harmony, you will never want to turn back.

INNER HARMONY EXERCISE

Ego or Soul?

When you are in recovery, especially in the beginning, it can be difficult to trust your motives. If your best thinking got you into trouble before, how do you differentiate between sane, spiritually-based thinking and dysfunctional, ego-driven reasoning? How do you determine whether you are operating out of fear and lack, or if your motives are grounded in a sense of love and wholeness? Are you making decisions from the highest place? It is a good idea to run important decisions by a sponsor or someone you trust, but the following exercise can teach you to identify your motives and determine whether your thoughts and actions come from your ego or your soul.

What you need:
- A few old magazines that feature beautiful people, upscale homes, cars, and so on. (You will need to rip out and cut pages, so be sure you no longer want the magazines.)
- Up to three photos of a friend, relative, or colleague you love or admire.
- A scissors, a timer, a dark magic marker, sticky notes, your journal, and a pen.

What to do:
1) Set the timer for ten minutes. Quickly thumb through the magazines searching for things you want: a gorgeous home, a great body, nice clothes, a beautiful face, a car, a glamorous life. You get the idea. Don't think about it. Just go with your first impulse and start ripping and cutting. (Be careful with the scissors, of course!) When the timer goes off, stop.

2) Look through the pictures. Be as honest as you can, and ask yourself why you want what's in the pictures. For example, if you've ripped out a picture of a beautiful home, ask if you want the home because you need a bigger house or love the beautiful architecture or if there's a deeper reason? Is there a feeling of lack? Do you believe a new home would somehow make you feel better about yourself, hide some flaw? Not every picture will spark this kind of reaction, but try to find at least one or two that do. See if you can identify any feelings of lack. Do you think you are not beautiful enough? Sophisticated enough? Powerful enough? Use the marker to write this feeling of lack on the picture. Go through the whole pile and do the same with the rest. Toss any pictures you didn't feel compelled to write on.

3) Next, spend five minutes looking at your personal photos. Look at the faces of the people you love or admire. How do they make you feel about yourself? Have you chosen a photo of a relative who encourages you? A teacher who made you feel smart? A friend who appreciates your sense of humor? Write how they make you feel on a sticky note, and place it on the photo.

4) Now place both sets of pictures on separate sides of a table. Look back and forth from one set to the other. Look at the words you've written. Notice how your feelings change when you move from one set of pictures to the other.

Take a deep breath and write for ten minutes, noting the quality of your feelings about one set of pictures and the other. Notice the difference between the feeling of lack and the feelings of love and wholeness.

When you have an important decision to make, use the memory of this exercise to help you determine whether you are operating from a sense of lack or from a more spiritual, loving place. Remember, this does not mean that you can't have new beautiful things or improve the way you look, and so forth. It is about being conscious of your motives, especially when you have difficult choices to make.

4

Tales of Transformation: Trent and Kim

*We must be willing to let go of
the life we have planned so as to have
the life that is waiting for us.*

—E. M. Forster

I F SOMEONE HAD WALKED UP TO ME twenty years ago and said, "Peter, one day you will teach meditation and yoga, chant in India, receive blessings from the Dalai Lama, and scour African forests for medicinal herbs," I would have stared in disbelief. Then I would have burst out laughing. There was no way I nor anyone else could have foreseen the transformation that would define the coming decades of my life.

But I am not an anomaly. I have seen astonishing shifts in people in recovery, especially those willing to invite a higher power into their lives through regular prayer and meditation. Two such people are Trent and Kim.* Both of them attended Twelve Step meetings for years, but still struggled to make conscious contact with a higher power of their understanding. They never stopped trying, though, and by the time they met me, they were eager to find a way to practice the Eleventh Step. Once they did, their recovery came to life in a new, dynamic way.

AA and other Twelve Step programs are described as fellowships "of men and women who share their experience, strength and hope with each other so that they may solve their common problem and help others recover." Here, Trent and Kim offer their own experience, strength, and hope about prayer and meditation. I include their courageous journeys here, so they might inspire you and affirm your own commitment to prayer and meditation.

Trent

 Trent, a fifty-eight-year-old state worker and divorced father of two adult sons, has been sober in AA for eight years.

"You're our only son, so you *have* to be somebody," my mother always said, a constant reminder that I was the only boy out of six children, and she had high expectations for me.

I never drank or did drugs in high school and was always active in sports. But when I got to college I was far from the golden boy my mother had dreamed of. I was always on the outside looking in. I felt so different. I had grown up in a small town and my father was an alcoholic. I had no idea what I was doing in college except that my sisters had gone there before me.

---

*Names and identifying information have been changed.

Finally Fitting In

I was nineteen the first time I got drunk. It was hard liquor and I puked. I was really happy though, because I finally felt like I fit in. Soon I discovered marijuana and loved that it made me feel articulate and profound. My circle of friends grew and we partied all the time. I was great at that part of college life. I was usually the last one to leave the keggers.

I paid my way through school waiting tables at a nearby resort. Unfortunately, this gave me access to more drugs and alcohol than any of my college friends had, so suddenly I was even more popular. I started experimenting with angel dust, Quaaludes, and acid, along with marijuana and lots of beer. I stopped going to most of my classes.

Somewhere along the line I got it into my head that if I could just meet a rich girl I would be motivated to make money. I didn't want *her* money; I just thought that a girl *from* money would inspire me. And that's what happened. I fell in love with Brenda, whose dad was a corporate executive on his way to being a millionaire.

My grades tanked, but I managed to eke out a 2.06 average, barely enough to put me over the 2.0 I needed to graduate. Brenda and I moved in together and kept on partying.

Marriage and Career

We married when I was twenty-four and she was nineteen. I had pretty low expectations of myself, but I knew I wanted to take care of my wife. When we were introduced to an international, multilevel sales and marketing company, everything changed. We actually started to make a go of it.

They didn't tolerate drinking or drugs, which was great because it kept me sober for six years. We started with nothing and within four years, I was in the upper 1 percent of income earners in the company. I went from country bumpkin to a guy with a nice house, cars, and a wife who always wore beautiful clothing. I was doing my mother proud, I thought.

The spending continued, though, and we gave no thought to managing our money. When business slowed, you would have never noticed because we kept on spending—far more than we made. And when I couldn't catch back up, my ego took a beating. In a pattern I was to repeat for years to come, I headed straight for a bar and kept going back. I tried hard to hide my drinking from the company, but in hindsight, it was pretty obvious what I was doing.

Living on Pins and Needles

I'd been drinking again for about a year when my first son was born. By then, the business had gone completely south, and in addition to drinking I was chasing women. My wife grew cold and distant, a great excuse for me to go to more bars looking for comfort in one-night stands.

I wore the mask of a successful businessman who had it together, but it was a complete lie. I had lost all sense of who I was. I lived on pins and needles. And I was not nice; I couldn't be. I could smile and say all the right words, but I was bound up with fear. My wife stopped trusting me and shut down completely. I owed so much money that we had to totally bail out of the business. In our best year, we'd had over a thousand distributors that I would address at conferences. Now we had nothing. I was lost, and dying, and I couldn't reach out for help.

As everything collapsed around me, the only thing I could think to do was leave town to save face. We moved, practically in the middle of the night, relocating to a city where my sister lived.

Dog and Pony Show

Even though I was broken inside, I could still sell and lie very well. I managed to land a job as a territory representative for a well-known tire company. They gave me the option of working in a larger market in a warm climate. We were drowning in debt and about to file for bankruptcy, so I jumped at it.

Ironically, not long after we arrived in our new town, a city council member knocked on our door. Apparently, our seemingly happy little family had given the growing community its 200,000th citizen. Here I was, the guy who had slipped out of town under the cover of night being written up as Mister-Wholesome-Family-Man on the front page of the local newspaper.

My wife was pregnant again, and we kept up our usual dog and pony show for the public. It was all a façade, though. Instead of going to work, I spent my days in bars and strip joints. My manager finally took me to task: "You're the sharpest, smartest guy we have here, but you're not doing your job." I couldn't even bring myself to work things out; I just resigned.

It was my pride. I had been raised to believe that you always had to be honest and have integrity, so as soon as my boss saw I wasn't living up to that standard, I quit. I couldn't handle failing him. If I didn't do the job well I didn't think I deserved to have it. I had sabotaged myself at my earlier job for similar reasons. When I figured out that the multilevel marketing was a scam,

I fell apart. Whenever I started compromising my principles, rather than figure out another way, I would completely self-destruct.

A Divorce

Up until then, I had been determined to save my marriage, but for the first time I knew it was over. We took a stab at counseling, but my wife and boys moved back north to live with my in-laws. This left me alone in our house with no job and nothing to do: a lethal combination. I got work doing construction with a bunch of illegal Irish workers. Immigration would storm through the work site, and then suddenly I'd be the only one left on the job. I'd turn around and guys would be sliding down drain pipes and hiding in chimneys. They all liked to drink and so did I. We partied, and I continued having flings with women.

At that point, the only saving grace in my life was a compassionate neighbor, Ron, who became something of a father figure. He didn't judge me, and for the first time in my life, I felt like I might be okay, no matter where I was or what I had done. His support was enough to give me some sense of who I was.

Another Start

I was thirty years old and decided I needed to move back north to be near my children and deal with the mountain of debt I'd amassed. I declared bankruptcy, moved in with my parents, and started over as a service manager for a car business. After a few years, I had a new relationship with my sons and my divorce was final. I was taking responsibility for my life and things were looking up.

The jobs got better. By now, I was responsible for thirty-eight employees, three managers, and millions of dollars in sales and inventory. The company was profitable, even winning a customer-satisfaction award. I thought everything was going to be okay, mostly because I'd figured out that I could drink daily *and* be functional . . . as long as I never drank at work.

But the more things went well, the more I got bored. Another pattern. Whenever I achieved anything, when I got to the point where I could take it easy and go golfing, so to speak, the challenge was over. Build it up and tear it down, a common pattern among all alcoholics, I later learned. I had straightened out six different dealerships then left them all.

The Downward Slide

The downward slide started again when I entered a very unhealthy relationship. I found out she was seeing another man and we ended it. I had cheated on my wife and remembered the look on her face when I told her about it. Now I understood exactly what she had felt. What goes around comes around, huh?

Now, at forty-three, I was drinking every day, rushing out of work just so I could go home and drink myself to sleep. My ex-wife called and said her second marriage was breaking up. Could the boys stay with me over the summer? I said absolutely. I realized how much my sons, now fifteen and seventeen, had needed their father, and I them.

By summer's end, my ex-wife's situation was still unresolved, so I moved to my sons' home state to take care of them while they finished school. For the first time in ages, I put myself aside and did what I thought was right. I cooked meals, took care of my boys, went to parent-teacher conferences, and even helped other kids in the neighborhood. But one thing I couldn't do was stop drinking.

I tried going to three AA meetings with my sister, who had been sober twenty years, and I stopped drinking for three days. After the third meeting I said, "Screw it."

But after my kids were out of the house and yet another relationship had fallen apart, I found myself alone and living in a trailer—something I had sworn I would never do. I spent my nights drinking from a thirty-pack of beer and staring at the TV. It got so bad I started to see the word *LOSER* pop up on the screen. I just could not stop drinking. I went to work hungover every morning.

Two or three times a week, I'd vow to stop drinking and dump my beer down the drain. But by the end of the night, I'd be shit-faced, drinking the last couple of beers from the thirty-pack. I'd wake up hungover again and go back to work. By 4 PM I'd be irritable and by 5 PM I'd be on the way to the beverage center for another thirty-pack. I'd crack one open on the car ride home and it would all start over. I had once promised myself I'd never drink in the morning, but now I was starting in first thing.

Finally, at age fifty, I found myself face to face with another frustrated, screaming boss and I walked out *again*. I wanted to die. I thought seriously about killing myself, but kept imagining my sons looking at me in the casket, saying, "Dad, we needed you." And I imagined how disappointed and guilty my mother and sisters would feel. Then, I remembered the AA meetings I'd gone to with my sister. So two days later, I contacted the intergroup hotline and I went. I haven't had a drink since.

Walking Through the Door at AA

As soon as I made the decision to walk in that door, I felt relief. Not that I wasn't shaky, but it was like coming home. I was on the pink cloud everyone talks about. I did what they suggested, ninety meetings in ninety days. I was broke, bankrupt again, but I went to meetings.

By then, I had burned every bridge in the car business. My AA friends told me to get a job, *any job*. I got one at a superstore unloading cargo. What would people think? What would *I* think? I went from earning six figures a year to seven-fifty an hour. I remember being so afraid of seeing someone I knew at the store that I would hide, sneaking around the aisles. I felt humiliated. But in hindsight, it was exactly what I needed to do to get back in the world while I went to meetings.

I was sober for a while, but completely uninterested in anything spiritual. I was just happy about not drinking. I'd been raised in the Presbyterian faith, and while I still felt I was a Christian, I was turned off by the shaming God I'd grown up with. Then I heard a guy share at a meeting. He was glowing and spoke from a place of truth. I really wanted to get to know him. It was Peter Amato. He kept saying, "The answers are within," and talked about "light" and "God," and I'd say, "What does that even *mean*?"

A Meditation Course

Peter invited me to sit in on a meditation course he was teaching for a county court drug program. At the time, meditation was completely foreign to me, a strange practice people from Eastern cultures did. But I wanted the promises of the program—"a new freedom and a new happiness." So, I tried it. It's not like I knew what I was looking for, but I'd made a decision to live a different way in recovery. I trusted Peter had come into my life for a reason.

From the start, I felt overwhelmed by the peace I experienced when I meditated with Peter. It was as if I had gotten a taste of a hot fudge sundae and wanted more; I knew I was just experiencing the tip of the iceberg. As I continued in the class, and as I got to know Peter, I was inspired to deepen my practice. Peter dealt with things so calmly; even during tax time, he was calm. It fascinated me. And after the hell I'd been through, I was truly open, willing, and ready.

Peter told our class, "If you pray and meditate thirty minutes every day for thirty days it will change your life." He started by teaching us to focus on our breath, to notice the moment of stillness between each inhalation and exhalation, and to watch thoughts pass like a parade or a cloud. He suggested we do this for fifteen minutes in the morning and fifteen minutes in the evening, and if we couldn't do it, to take less time, but just to start.

An Energy Shift

It took me a couple of sessions to get into it. It was very hard to sit there. Peter told me it would be like that. For the first week, I could only do fifteen minutes a day, but then I made a decision to do the full thirty minutes every day in spite of myself. I don't know how it happened, but after the fourth day my energy started to shift, fear and anxiety went away. I felt more at peace, and I wanted to continue to the end of the thirty days.

I'm a person whose mind was always busy, but I started to feel a sense of space in my thinking and in my life. Sometimes the fifteen minutes would be over and I'd completely lost track of ten minutes of it; I'd stopped thinking.

I began to realize that not only is there space between breaths, but there is space or gaps between thoughts. Until then, my brain and my mouth were connected. I came to understand that I could spend time in that space if I chose and not be at the mercy of every thought that went by.

Running on Intuition

AA's "Promises" (found in the "Big Book") talk about "intuitively knowing how to handle problems which used to baffle us." I started to notice that as I went about my day I had intuition about how to handle things. I wasn't *trying* to figure things out; I just was figuring things out. Instead of reacting right away, I would actually give things time. I didn't have to constantly plan and scheme, because I started to trust that things were working themselves out. I stopped getting caught up in the drama of life.

After the thirty days, I really started to like myself, to feel okay in my own skin. I had tapped into my source, and there is nothing bigger than that. I felt like I'd come home. Once you experience that, you just know you're okay. But if you stop praying and meditating, you feel the difference. You start sliding into an old, anxious, irritable disconnected place.

I found that when I live this way, I become more ordinary— in a good way. It's not so important to be right, to be number one, to have an agenda. I don't have to have a comment every time someone speaks or be the focus of attention. I exist instead of having to be in the forefront.

Today, I practice prayer and meditation four or five days a week for a minimum of fifteen minutes. Sometimes I sit for thirty minutes, sometimes forty-five. I don't set timeframes anymore. Sometimes, out of nowhere, I'll just do a meditation. Something is bothering me, and I think, *Oh, you could sit now.* Your practice becomes part of who you are.

Much to Discover

Prayer and meditation have really changed my life, brought an inner peace that is remarkable. To this day, even if I don't meditate daily, I can still go back to that state. I can quiet my mind, breathe, and still know everything is okay. Intuition is always there if I keep practicing. It puts me on a higher plane.

But I still have much to discover. God is that big. Before recovery I was always in search of the eternal buzz, and there was never enough. But I've learned that God is bigger than any thirst I have. God and light come into me. I drank and used drugs to lower my consciousness. Now, I *want* to be aware; I *want* to be conscious.

My New Life

Eventually, I became so immersed in my practice, so excited to be part of the community Peter formed in our area, that when he went out of town one winter, I taught his meditation program myself. I also took over the regular practice sessions he offered at the county court program and in our community. I haven't taught for a while, but I feel inspired to return to it again because I am always moved by what happens when I bring this message to people in recovery. In my experience, no one who makes a deliberate commitment to a spiritual life slips backward.

Today, I am gainfully employed. I work in a civil service position and my relationship with my sons is excellent. All my relationships have healed; I'm not confrontational anymore. I don't have an agenda. I don't create a lot of resistance in my life. I also don't make a ton of money now, but I'm okay. I can honestly say that I really like who I am. I've developed enough humility, had my ego deflated enough, to tie in with a higher power.

Today, I know that almost anything I perceive to be a problem is simply a mirror telling me there's something going on inside me that I'm not accepting. I don't have the urge to drink or drug anymore, though sometimes I do notice TV ads for beer. When that happens, I know I am off. When I have those moments, I know I need to get quiet and sit, journal, and get to an AA meeting. That's meditation. That's the gift of awareness I've received.

Kim's Story

Kim is a forty-six-year-old healthcare administrator with eighteen years of sobriety in AA. She started drinking when she was fifteen years old. Despite binges and blackouts, she managed to hold her life together through graduate school and a successful career, but the day she orchestrated an intervention for her brother she realized she had a problem of her own.

My father's death certificate listed several causes of death; one of them was cirrhosis of the liver. I grew up in a large family and no one ever talked about my dad's alcoholism. I started drinking when I was fifteen, and then when he died I had no idea how to process it. So I turned to alcohol even more.

Just a Weekend Warrior

By the time I was eighteen, I had been arrested three times for underage drinking. I smoked pot, too, but alcohol was always my drug of choice. At age twenty-two, I got married . . . to an alcoholic, of course. We had a relationship based on drinking, so things went from bad to worse. I always managed to look okay to the world, but inside I was a mess, bingeing on weekends with beer, rum and cokes, and Alabama slammers. I fooled myself into believing it was okay, that I was just a "weekend warrior."

I didn't think it was strange that I couldn't wait to get wasted and black out.

Things kept going downhill. I couldn't handle the stress of everyday life. I was worried all the time. Worried what people thought of me; worried that I wasn't doing enough; worried that I wasn't enough. I was a doer. I could never let myself be. I always had to be busy.

I went to school to earn my masters, but things got so bad I couldn't concentrate on my homework. I remember losing my mind the day of an exam. I was so anxious about taking the test that I screamed at everyone: at my husband, even my boss. I exploded and told my boss he was giving me too much responsibility.

Someone Else's Fault

Of course, everything at that time was someone else's fault. I was never accountable for anything that happened to me. I was always sure I was unhappy because of stress at my job, or because my husband had done something to me.

Needless to say, my marriage was over in eight years. But I would never let anyone know how much I was hurting. I prided myself on looking good on the outside. My brother, however, was a mess. His life had fallen apart. He was definitely an alcoholic. I was so worried about him that, in my usual doer mode, I organized an intervention.

I remember scrambling around, frenetic, trying to orchestrate my brother's salvation, making sure family members and therapists were available and ready. Little did I know that I was actually organizing my own intervention, too.

An Alcoholic Is Me

When the big day arrived, my mind was racing. I was so stressed out by logistics and family dynamics that the intervention counselor actually took me aside to suggest I might also have a problem. It didn't take much convincing. I knew immediately that he was right.

I was relieved when he suggested I do some writing on the question "What is an alcoholic?" I remember the last sentence I wrote: "An alcoholic is me." By the time I took my last two drinks, I knew *I just can't do this any more.* It was a powerful feeling for someone like me, someone who always had to have the right answers to finally say *I don't know* to the universe.

Ironically, I ended up in the same rehab with my brother, although we went through treatment separately. I finished twenty-nine days then went to ninety AA meetings in ninety days. Three and a half years into recovery, the compulsion to drink had left me, but emotionally and spiritually, I was still stuck. I knew my soul needed some nourishment to feel happy, joyous, and free, but I'd been turned off to religion and had never given much thought to prayer and meditation.

When I met Peter, I had actually been sober longer than he had. It seemed as if he'd just come into the program, but Peter grew and changed so quickly that I was immediately interested in what he was doing. I'd been exposed to some yoga and to spiritual tapes, but had had a hard time making prayer and meditation a part of my daily life. It was not until Peter started some meditation groups at his wellness center that I began exploring spirituality more deeply. I also attended some of his retreats.

Clear the Clutter

Peter had a new and refreshing way of talking about prayer and meditation. I learned that meditation is not about what we think, it's about *stopping* the thinking process, being in the present moment. I learned how to clear the clutter in my mind, to turn it off. Even though I had been on a few retreats here and there, Peter brought meditation right into my community. It became accessible. Suddenly, I was not just meditating and praying once a year, but practicing regularly.

It was an amazing time. I had really struggled with meditation on my own, had difficulty quieting my mind. But I learned how to do it. I became comfortable. Soon, prayer and meditation became an essential part of my life and the key to keeping me sober. It took discipline to stick with it, but these practices are the core of my spiritual life today and the source of my spiritual growth. I learned that prayer allows me to dialogue with my higher power, and meditation allows me to hear my higher power's answers. The answers I get are not always what I want them to be, and sometimes no answer can be the answer.

My Practice

In the beginning, I started small and worked my way up to an hour each day. Today, I don't always do a formal meditation, but most days I go to a peaceful room in my house that I've dedicated for prayer and meditation, and I spend some kind of quiet time there, usually fifteen minutes in the morning and fifteen minutes in the evening. Sometimes I write in a journal. When I'm stressed, I turn to prayer and meditation to find God's will. I also love being outdoors and often use that time as my meditation. I can be walking, kayaking, just enjoying living in the present moment.

Today, I get serenity and peace of mind from prayer and meditation and from living a spiritual life. My practice allows me to live in the moment and on life's terms. My mother passed away in August 2009 and my spiritual connection helped me through the grief. I realized that we are all human beings having a spiritual experience; that we are just passing through here onto something better.

Then and Now

Looking back, I see so many contrasts in my life between who I used to be and who I am now. There is less time for drama. I know I'm okay now. If other people sometimes look at me like I'm crazy, it doesn't bother me. I'm good with who I am and what I do. If other people want to judge that, it's okay. I accept who and what I am. I take my time and I take care of myself.

Today, my fear is gone, and I know that there is a God and he is taking care of me. I know how to feel the love, peace, serenity, and calmness that meditation brings. I always know things will be okay. To the person who is just beginning on this path, I would tell them to keep working at it, to try different methods—sitting, walking meditation, or whatever works for you. The bottom line is, if you want to have a great life, prayer and meditation should be part of it.

As you can see, Trent and Kim worked hard to find a connection to a higher power of their understanding. It did not happen overnight. It was a process—a combination of education, willingness, and a commitment to practice. But their work paid off. Today, when I stand face to face with these two special people, I feel their serenity and connectedness to a higher source.

As Kim pointed out, when she practices the Eleventh Step "there is less time for drama" and more time to enjoy the gifts of life previously obscured by misguided, addictive thinking. And as Kent said, it is rare that anyone who embraces the Eleventh Step slips backward. In fact, most people who embrace prayer and meditation in recovery move forward in a positive, productive, and surprising manner. That is not to say a spiritual path is without pain or struggle. But when you have a framework in which to handle life's problems, when you have a spiritual practice, solutions arrive faster, and situations resolve more easily. Trent and Kim are living proof of this.

INNER HARMONY EXERCISE

Your Own Transformation

Other people's tales of transformation can be inspiring. Taking stock of your own story—your own transformation—can be just as inspiring and even educational.

What you need: A photograph of yourself that is at least two years old (one you remember taking), your journal, and a pen.

What to do: Spend a minute looking at the photograph of yourself. Take a deep breath and try to remember how you felt the day it was taken. If you can't remember your feelings that day, try to remember how you generally felt during that period. Specifically try to recall any fears or insecurities. Write down as many of those feelings as you can. If you have trouble identifying feelings, try to intuit them from your body language in the picture. Are your arms crossed? Shoulders tense? Are you smiling? Frowning? And if that fails, guess what your emotions might have been. It might sound strange, but the mind is powerful. So, even if you cannot remember the day, or if you were emotionally disconnected from feelings at the time, you have internal wisdom that is likely to provide you with answers.

Review the list and place a check mark next to any fears or insecurities that are still with you today. Focus on them for a minute. Have these fears or insecurities changed at all? Even a little? Observe what you've written but don't judge or criticize.

Next, put a star next to any fears and insecurities that are gone. Think about what changed. Why do you feel differently? How were you transformed? Use this to learn about the way you transform.

Did you do something to bring about this shift? Did something happen to you?

Give yourself credit for all the work you have done to grow. Express gratitude to your higher power for helping you become the person you are today.

PART TWO:

Prayer
and
Meditation

5

INNER HARMONY PRAYER AND MEDITATION

Be at least as interested in what goes on inside you as what happens outside. If you get the inside right, the outside will fall into place.

—Eckhart Tolle

IN AA'S "BIG BOOK," *Alcoholics Anonymous*, we are told that sobriety is a "daily reprieve" contingent on staying in "fit spiritual condition." This means the gift of sobriety or abstinence depends on our ability to maintain a connection to a higher power *one day at a time*. In other words, the gifts of the program depend on our *conscious choice* to reach out to a higher power each day. If we become complacent and forget to make this contact, our recovery can quickly suffer. The Eleventh Step suggests using prayer and meditation to improve this contact with our higher power.

Prayer and meditation are ancient practices that can be executed in as many ways as there are people, religions, and spiritual traditions. But for our purposes, we use prayer and meditation to quiet the mind—so we can "hear" direction from a power greater than ourselves, find guidance within, and gain strength to act on it.

So, what are prayer and meditation, and how do we practice them?

Prayer

When we pray as directed by the Eleventh Step, we are not praying in the traditional sense. We do not ask God, nature, the universe, or our higher power to fulfill a specific desire or need. The Eleventh Step suggests we pray *only* for knowledge of our higher power's will for us—that we ask this higher power to help us find wisdom and direction on what our next right thought or action should be.

The step also directs us to pray for *strength* to act on the guidance we receive. We need this strength because the message we receive sometimes requires difficult action. For example, if you prayed about coming clean about a lie, you might receive guidance that an apology is in order. However, making that apology—admitting you are wrong and facing the consequences of that admission—might demand more strength than you can muster. Praying to a higher power for strength can help you take on difficult but spiritually sound actions. Your prayer acknowledges that, left to your own devices, you might want to take the easier way out. But when you ask for strength, it usually arrives. You discover that extra bit of moral courage you need to do the right thing. This is your intention when you pray. This is *how* to pray.

Prayer in Action

To put prayer into action, begin by sitting on a meditation cushion, unrolling a yoga mat, or even looking at a beautiful sunset and asking for guidance. In a sense, carving out time for contemplation is a prayer in itself. It demonstrates your willingness to move beyond old ideas and beliefs.

When you rise in the morning, you might ask what your higher power's will is for you that day, or you can be more specific, asking for direction for a new path in life, or for insight into how to handle a particular situation.

It is best to phrase your request for guidance in a clear, concise manner. For example, if you're considering changing jobs, you might say: "Please show me where and how I might best serve you and others, using my talents, knowledge, and skill. Please give me the strength to hear you and follow your guidance." Whatever phrase you choose, repeat it silently or aloud a few times then let it go. You have set your intention. You have asked for guidance; now it is out of your hands.

Remember, we all have answers we'd *like* to hear, but the Eleventh Step suggests letting go of our "best thinking." In this state of mind we are ready to meditate.

Meditation

We've talked about the ego, how ruthless it can be, especially for someone struggling to overcome addiction. The ego can bombard you with resentments and worry. It can scrape and claw to distract you from the here and now so you act against your own health and well-being. In Eastern traditions, this kind of thinking is often called "monkey mind." Thoughts leap from one extreme to the other like a frenetic primate swinging from tree to tree in a wild, overgrown jungle.

When we meditate, we focus our attention on one thought, movement, sound, task, or thing for an extended period of time, thereby quieting this monkey mind. The object of our focus can be the breath, the sensations of a yoga pose, the vibrations of a mantra, an image, counting beads, and so on. This is sometimes called *mindfulness meditation,* because we let the mind rest in a single spot or activity, clearing extraneous thought for a period of time. Mindfulness meditation is a powerful tool that gives you the ability, in any moment, to quiet your mind, ground yourself in the present, and listen for guidance.

Sitting Meditation

We'll begin with a form of sitting meditation that involves remaining quiet as you pay attention to the steady flow of air in and out of your lungs. In Chapter 9, we'll explore more physically active forms of meditation, including yoga, sound work, and walking meditation. But for now, become acquainted with your breath. Remember, you are trying to quiet your mind and move beyond thought so you can connect with the wisdom of the universe inherent in stillness.

Preparation

To begin your sitting meditation, you will need a quiet spot where you feel certain you will not be interrupted. This can be a room, a corner, or even a chair. You can fill this space with pictures of people or things you love, or of someone you admire such as a teacher, mentor, or anyone who possesses qualities you want to cultivate in yourself. The idea is to make your meditation area welcoming and full of positive associations so you want to return to it daily. If you can, set a regular time for your practice. But if that's not possible, begin by carving out at least a minute or two at some point each day.

If children or other family members distract you, try setting a timer for them, letting them know that you cannot be disturbed until the bell rings. This creates a clear, easily understood boundary and eliminates anxiety about being interrupted.

You can sit on the floor or use a chair. If you opt for the floor, you might be more comfortable using a meditation cushion, pillow, or folded blanket tucked under your tailbone. You can cross your legs or not. If you suffer from back pain or are uncomfortable on the ground, a chair is preferable.

The most important thing is that you sit in an upright position with an emphasis on a straight spine and neck. Your pelvis should be tipped slightly forward and your chest and heart open. Imagine a string is holding you up through the crown of your head. Proper alignment allows energy to flow openly through your body.

Breathing on Purpose

If you are blessed with good health, your breath—the steady flow of air in and out of your lungs—has been with you since birth. Sometimes it is fast and shallow, other times slow and deep. But it is always there, in and out, steady and true.

Most of us take our breath for granted, and rightly so. Our bodies are programmed to ignore it. Our autonomic nervous system regulates breathing and other bodily functions including our heartbeat, digestion, perspiration, and salivation. They are involuntary. We don't have to think about them. But unlike our heartbeat, we can control our breath for brief periods. We can start our breath, stop it, speed it up, or slow it down at will. This makes the breath a useful tool for learning to focus the mind.

We also have an amazing ability to place our awareness anywhere we want it to go. We can use our minds to travel around our own bodies, to transport ourselves across the globe, and to imagine things that are absurd, horrific, beautiful, or fantastic. Whatever we want. We can *decide* where we want to put our attention and when. This is the miracle of human thought and consciousness.

In sitting meditation, we deliberately place our focus where we want it. In this case, we return our attention to our breath over and over again. The mind will definitely wander—that is its nature—but our practice is to continually return our attention to the sensation of the breath. I think of this type of meditation as *breathing on purpose.*

If we continue this practice for longer and longer periods of time—returning our attention to the breath over and over again no matter what distracts us—we soon sink into deeper and deeper states of consciousness. We experience a sense of peace.

In this state, our minds become like radio receivers. We can hear our inner wisdom and witness our own minds. We begin to see thoughts, feelings, and emotions come and go. We can see that we don't have to attach ourselves to our thoughts. We can watch them arise and fade away. Once we begin to master this *witness consciousness,* we gain the ability to decide, in any moment, where we want to put our attention.

Just as a pianist practices scales to master a musical composition, we practice the simple action of focusing on our breath over and over again to master the art of thinking clearly and sanely. If your mind tells you to act in self-destructive ways, you can use the awareness you develop in meditation to gently but firmly move your attention back to positive, productive, or spiritual thoughts.

Remember, when you meditate your mind *will* wander. Your practice is to gently and lovingly bring your attention back to the breath, over and over. *I have to pick up some groceries,* your mind says. Gently return to the breath. *The mortgage is due.* Breathe in and out. *My boss thinks I'm lazy.* Return your attention to the breath. *Is my relationship in trouble?* Over and over, back to the breath.

You want to approach meditation with the same love, joy, and compassion you would give a toddler learning to walk. Just like a child, you are stumbling along, trying something new and difficult. There is nothing to beat yourself up about; no judgments or criticism are necessary.

Focus Points

Take a deep breath. In, then out. In and out. Where is the first place you feel air moving? At the opening of the nostrils? In the nasal passages? On the upper lip? Or is the rising and falling of your abdomen the strongest sensation when you breathe? Wherever you feel the act of breathing first, simply notice it. Place your attention there. Let go and relax. Try doing this for a minute. If you can do this with relative ease, go for longer and longer periods.

Mindfulness is about embracing the present moment and quieting the mind long enough to "hear" the voice of a higher power within. Certainly, it is a challenge to bring your mind back to your breath repeatedly, especially when thoughts—negative or positive—fight for your attention. But remember, meditation is never about punishing yourself. It is about learning compassion and patience, about being gentle and kind. It is just as important to cultivate these qualities as it is to learn how to keep your focus.

In the beginning, you can expect intense feelings and thoughts to arise. You might even want to quit. You may think, *If I can't do it perfectly, why do it at all?* But I promise you can survive the thoughts and the feelings. Use the tool of prayer to ask for the strength to continue. Lovingly acknowledge your ego's desire to keep you safe by reminding you of all the things you need to do, but gently guide your attention back to your breath. Eventually, your ego will relax, know you will be okay, and let you ease into beautiful, meditative silence.

As I have said, I recommend that you practice mindfulness meditation every day for fifteen minutes in the morning and evening. If you can't sit for that long, don't worry—simply do what you can. You can also use a recorded, guided meditation (see the Inner Harmony exercise at the end of this chapter). The main thing is to minimize your frustration so you *want* to return to your practice every day.

After you pray and meditate, remain open to insight, ideas, and inspiration. Treat each meditation as a joyful ride. You never know what gifts or surprises will arrive when you are done.

The Science of Addiction and Mindfulness

If you are an atheist or agnostic and are uncomfortable thinking of meditation in spiritual terms, you might find it helpful to know that there is a scientific basis for using meditation as a tool for overcoming addiction.

During the past two decades, many researchers who specialize in addiction treatment have taken notice of mindfulness meditation. G. Alan Marlatt, Ph.D., coauthor of *Mindfulness-Based Relapse Prevention: A Clinician's Guide,* studies the effectiveness of mindfulness meditation for the prevention of addiction relapse. He defines mindfulness meditation as the practice of sustained attention and nonjudgmental awareness of the mind and body.

In a recent pilot study that Marlatt and his colleagues conducted at the Addictive Behaviors Research Center at the University of Washington, relapse rates of recovering alcoholics and addicts in a standard prevention program (which included voluntary access to Twelve Step programs) were compared to those of recovering addicts in a similar program that included mindfulness meditation.

The results demonstrated that 85 percent of the patients in the regular program relapsed after one year, compared to only 40 percent of those who participated in the meditation-based program. In an interview for this book, Martlatt concluded that "people trained in mindfulness do much better. There's less relapse and drug use compared to treatment as usual."

The Mechanics of Addiction

M. Kathleen B. Lustyk, Ph.D., a professor of psychology at Seattle Pacific University's School of Psychology, Family, and Community is one of Marlatt's colleagues. She explained that drugs and alcohol impact the brain's mesolimbic system, which regulates pleasure through the neurotransmitter dopamine. "When an animal is given just one dose of alcohol, methamphetamine, or cocaine their pathways get turned on. Just one dose, and the brain goes 'Wow that was great. How do I get more?'"

Drugs and alcohol stimulate the base of the brain, which then sends signals to a higher region where pleasure registers and behavior is learned. A *pleasure circuit* forms that prompts the mind to repeat these good feelings by seeking out and using a desired substance. Lustyk said this pattern continues in a *positive feedback system* until the pleasure circuit gets "hijacked."

Putting on the Brakes

Enter mindfulness meditation. Lustyk said meditation affects the brain's prefrontal cortex (located behind the forehead). This area regulates impulse control and emotions. "It's where we plan and decide whether and when to act," she said, adding that in a healthy person, the prefrontal cortex "does a lovely job of toning down the pleasure circuit or managing emotions going awry." However, in addicts the same region physically shrinks and becomes ineffective.

"What's so beautiful about mindfulness meditation is that it tackles the primary parts of this system. It *turns on* the prefrontal cortex. For a substance abuser, it's a way of activating the brakes over this cycle."

In 2005, a groundbreaking study by Harvard researcher Sara W. Lazar showed that mindfulness meditation not only stimulates the prefrontal cortex, it actually *thickens* it.

Lustyk believes Lazar's findings have positive implications for people who struggle with addiction. The research shows "there was this beautiful thickening happening in the brains of meditators, which is the very part that is damaged by addiction." And meditation affects the brain quickly. "Do a breath awareness exercise and the prefrontal part of the cortex turns on and peripheral markers of stress are reduced. We may come to find that there are long-term benefits from a mini-meditation."

Both Marlatt and Lustyk said that the "brake" effect meditation provides allows addicts to put mental "space" between their feelings and reactions. For example, Lustyk said, someone struggling with cravings can take a moment to label their feelings before they act. "They can say to themselves: *this is anxiety, I'm stressed.* Research shows that when you give an emotion a label, you actually turn on other parts of the prefrontal cortex that work with the braking response."

A Feeling of Oneness

Psychiatrist Reef Karim, M.D., another researcher in the field of addiction, says meditation not only puts the brakes on cravings it "shuts down" the parietal lobe, at the back of the brain. This creates the feeling of oneness that many meditators experience. Karim is founder and medical director of the Control Center in Beverly Hills, an outpatient facility for patients struggling with a wide range of behavioral issues such as sex addiction, spending issues, and video game and Internet addiction. He also treats people with chemical addictions and is assistant clinical professor at UCLA's Semel Institute for Neuroscience and Human Behavior. According to Dr. Karim:

> *When activated, the parietal lobe is where you process information about space and time; it orients you to the uniqueness of you. It determines where the rest of the world is and where you are. Diminishing activity in this area produces a feeling of being one with the universe from a brain standpoint. The ego is such a huge issue for addicts that if there is a way you can spiritually or mechanically shut down or minimize the ego, that's a good thing.*

The Future of Addiction Treatment

Lustyk, Marlatt, and Karim envision mindfulness meditation playing a significant role in the future of addiction treatment. If research continues to prove mindfulness meditation is an effective tool for people struggling with addiction, Marlatt believes treatment will look very different in the future: "If meditation shows itself to be more effective [than traditional treatment] in the long run, it will revolutionize the field."

INNER HARMONY EXERCISE

Guided Meditations

Below are transcripts of two guided meditations that are available as recordings at www.soulsilencethebook.com. However, I include them here because it can be very powerful to record these meditations in your own voice for your practice. You might add soothing music in the background. Guided meditations are useful if you have a lot of difficulty quieting your mind.

You can also use these meditations in a group setting. Some people find it is easier to sink into a meditative state when they are in a group. If your friends or family members express interest in meditation, I recommend getting together with them once or twice a week and taking turns leading the session by reading one or both of the meditations below.

Guided Meditation #1 (fifteen minutes)

In this session, we will dwell in silence for fifteen minutes. It will be most effective if you can find the willingness to surrender to just being here now, forgetting about the question of time. Gently allowing your eyes to close, becoming in touch with your awareness and then your breathing. Feeling the cool air moving up and through your nose, and the warmer air gently departing. Noticing your belly rise and fall as you sit with yourself in stillness. Breathing. Knowing that you are breathing. Being available to feel each breath arrive. In and out. Listening, deeply, to the silence under the breath. If you find you have drifted away from observing your breathing to a thought or emotion, simply note it and gently escort your awareness back to the feeling of the next inhale. Moving in now even closer on stillness and the present moment. Fully in your body. Feeling the waves of breath gently massaging your body and mind. Checking to see if your mind is focused on your breathing right now. Feeling the rhythm of its pulsations. Breathing. Knowing that you are breathing. Breathing on purpose. Closing in on the silence between my words. Only you and your breath . . .

(SILENCE)

And as we move toward completion, drop an intention into your awareness for your eyes to drift open, listening in on the silence, and basking in the stillness you have cultivated for yourself. Taking a mental snapshot, knowing you can hang on to, recall, or rekindle this peace whenever your beautiful heart desires.

Guided Meditation #2 (thirty minutes)

In this session, we will dwell in silence for thirty minutes. Let us allow it to be an opportunity for looking deeply, allowing yourself the time to engage in this practice of nondoing. Taking time for you to establish an upright, seated posture, with an emphasis on aligning the spine and neck, as though there is a string holding up the crown of your head. Moving toward an acceptance of slowing down time. Allowing your eyes to drift closed and getting in touch with your breath. Admiring it like a wave of completeness, filling you and then emptying itself, as if using you as a container to hold itself in. Becoming aware of breathing in and out through your nose. Feeling the cool air entering and the warmer air departing. Be there with the breath when the inhale flips over and turns into an exhale. Simply observing the space between the in and the out. The idea here is to witness your breathing with awareness. To get in touch with who is actually doing the breathing. If and when you notice that your mind has drifted off to a thought, simply note it and gently escort your mind back to the feeling of the next inhale. Without judgment. Breathing, knowing that you are breathing. Just with this breath. And this one. Continuing to go under the thoughts, finding contentment and harmony. Through the pulsing of breath and the rhythm of the wave. Realizing how deep this nourishment actually feels. Becoming satisfied and fulfilled. Just sitting. Breathing. Even smiling to yourself. Following the entire path of the inhale and the exhale. Each time there is a cycle. Knowing you are with it, breath after breath. Allowing the breath to ground you in the present moment. Returning to the inhale, allow your awareness to scan your physical body and mental field to more or less check in on yourself. Noticing if you are holding on to any thought or any physical tightness or sense of anxiety as you dwell in stillness. Allowing and embracing any of these spots or areas as part of the process. Breathing in and out of any tight or painful areas with awareness, as well as allowing the thoughts to just scan by. Not having to attach or grasp at any one thought or feeling. Staying solid with the breath and its rhythm. Allowing it to be enough to sustain you in any given moment. Simply bathing you in peace and contentment. Wave by wave. Being aware of the flow of your breath. Simply present with whatever occurs from breath to breath. Not judging or attaching. Simply breathing past it. Sitting, knowing that you are sitting. Releasing and relaxing on each exhale. Fully present. Not thinking. Actually listening in on the silence. Continuing to dwell in stillness. In silence. Moment by moment. Breath by breath. Returning the mind back to the sensations of breath. The memory of just being fully present with the breath. Gently moving in your body and out of your body.

(SILENCE)

As your meditation session comes to an end, take a moment to feel your body pulsating, to acknowledge the calm in your being. Enjoy the nourishment you have given yourself through intention and nondoing. Know that you have been brave enough to see yourself exactly as you are as a human being. Remember how good this feels so you want to come back to your meditation practice time and again.

As you develop your meditation skills, a whole new way of living will unfold. You will learn that genuine happiness can only reside in each and every one of your present moments. All you have to do is be there.

6

FACING LIFE'S UPS
AND DOWNS

*How people treat you is their karma;
how you react is yours.*

—Dr. Wayne Dyer

PRAYER AND MEDITATION provide guidance and spiritual sustenance to some of the world's most influential leaders. Two such men are the Dalai Lama—the exiled political and spiritual leader of Tibet and a Nobel laureate, and Thich Nhat Hanh—a Buddhist monk, poet, teacher, and Nobel Prize nominee who was exiled from his native Vietnam for protesting the war there in the 1960s and '70s.

These devoutly spiritual men are my teachers and heroes, and I have been blessed to meet them both. In 2000, I partnered with the Smithsonian Institute to bring the Dalai Lama to Washington,

D.C., for the museum's Folklife Festival. There, I was honored to receive his private blessings. In 1998, I studied meditation with Nhat Hanh, who ordained me as a member of his Order of Interbeing, a community dedicated to the study, practice, and observance of fourteen mindfulness precepts.

For anyone on a spiritual path, the Dalai Lama and Thich Nhat Hanh offer powerful lessons about the part mindfulness can play in handling life's ups and downs. They are living examples that a commitment to spiritual principles does not guarantee a life free of hardship or pain, but that practicing prayer and meditation connects you to a higher power, which, in turn, gives you wisdom and strength to make informed choices about how to face difficulties. When you incorporate spiritual practices into your daily life, as these great men have, you learn to handle challenges with grace, dignity, and understanding.

Enlightened Men Have Feelings Too

In the 1950s, the Dalai Lama fled Tibet after the Chinese government slaughtered thousands of his followers and stole his country from beneath his feet. Thich Nhat Hanh witnessed the senseless killing during the Vietnam War and was banished from his country after he protested his government's role in that conflict.

Such hardships might have destroyed, or at least embittered, most human beings, but neither man has let persecution, misfortune, or cruelty dampen his spirits or derail his work. Both have drawn on their extensive spiritual training and deep connection to a higher source to become stronger and more determined, to dedicate their lives to helping others, and to bring a message of peace, kindness, and unswerving love to the world.

At the same time, neither Thich Nhat Hanh nor the Dalai Lama has ever claimed he is above anger, grief, or despair. In fact, in an interview with *Life Positive* magazine, the Dalai Lama said negative emotions are a regular part of his life. However, he explained that he has learned to process such feelings and move beyond them. For example, he spoke in detail about how to handle anger:

> If you are able to recognize the moment when anger arises you will be able to distinguish the part of your mind that is feeling anger. This will divide your mind in two parts—one part will be feeling anger while the other will be trying to observe. Therefore, anger cannot dominate the entire mind. You are able to recognize that anger is harmful and maybe develop an antidote to it. View your anger objectively. Try to see the positive side of the anger-causing person or event.

Similarly, Nhat Hanh, in an interview for *O* magazine, said he was not immune to upset or discord. He said he was "angry, worried, sad, hurt" after his exile from Vietnam in 1966. Like the Dalai Lama, Hanh offered insight into the way he processed his feelings, specifically fear:

> You embrace it tenderly and look deeply into it. And as you embrace your pain, you get relief and you find out how to handle that emotion . . . then you have enough insight in order to solve the

problem. The problem is to not allow that anxiety to take over. When these feelings arise, you have to practice in order to use the energy of mindfulness to recognize them, embrace them, and look deeply into them. It's like a mother when the baby is crying. Your anxiety is your baby. You have to take care of it. You have to go back to yourself, recognize the suffering in you, embrace the suffering, and you get relief. And if you continue with your practice of mindfulness, you understand the roots, the nature of the suffering, and you know the way to transform it.

In other words, no matter how enlightened you become, you still have emotions. The measure of your recovery and spiritual growth is how you process them.

Motivation to Delve Deeper

When I met the Dalai Lama and Thich Nhat Hanh, I experienced a sense of peace in their presence that is difficult to convey; the depth of their connection to a spiritual source was palpable. In times of stress or doubt, I often draw strength by remembering that feeling and by acknowledging the fortitude, wisdom, and moral resolve both men have exhibited in the face of terrible trauma, struggle, and persecution.

While my own struggles have never approached the kind of epic hardships that the Dalai Lama and Nhat Hanh have endured, I have faced my share of doubt, skepticism, and condescension. When I began my quest more than a decade ago to introduce integrative medicine into my community and to doctors' offices and hospitals, I had to convince members of the medical establishment that there is wisdom in treating the entire human rather than just his or her symptoms. Not being a doctor myself, I was often met with a chilly reception, to put it politely.

Similarly, when I offered prayer and meditation groups in my community, and when I suggested that a state prison and local courts offer meditation and stress reduction programs to their populations, the laughter was often audible. I even tried to convince the school board of my blue-collar community that students would not only benefit from a daily meditation program, but would enjoy it. Talk about stone faces.

Of course, behind the skepticism I recognized enough interest to push on. But I can tell you that there were plenty of times I was filled with doubt. *Am I crazy?* I would wonder. *Maybe they're right. Do I continue investing time, money, and energy into something no one wants or understands, and get abused on top of it?* I remember thinking, *I don't need this. I can go and retire!* Even after years of spiritual study, I faced a daily inner battle; it was a challenge not to get upset, angry, and downright pissed off.

But instead of giving up, I used those feelings as motivation to delve deeper into my spiritual practice, to remain authentic to who I was and what I dreamed was possible.

An Opportunity to Improve

I learned that if I can remain conscious about my own feelings and the reactions of the people around me, I don't have to take things personally. It is in difficult moments—when I'm tweaked or annoyed—that my many years of prayer and meditation pay off. Just as I have learned to let my thoughts and feelings move through me during meditation—returning to my breath, mantra, or the sensations of a yoga pose, over and over again—so, too, have I learned to watch my emotions come and go in times of distress. My feelings, just like my breath, rise and fall away.

I know I can always take a breath in the moment, experience the power of a divine presence within, and move beyond fear, anger, or frustration. Rather than shutting down or cutting people off, I have learned to use difficult experiences to recognize that one or both of us has become disconnected from the truth.

I ask myself questions like: *Do the people doubting me need more information? Is there any chance this person is open to my message or is my energy better spent elsewhere? Is there an opportunity to improve the way I present my point of view?*

I do not always remain conscious; I am human. But such moments are fewer and farther between. And when I don't show up as my highest self in a situation, I can always process my feelings later in the day. It is never too late.

Handling a Real-Life Situation

So what can you do when the world won't go your way, when your needs go unmet? Let's say you just worked very hard on a project for your job. You turned it in to your boss and he or she zeroed in on a mistake. Naturally, you felt "dissed" or negated; your pride was hurt.

The first thing to recognize is that discomfort has kicked in because one or both of you is operating out of an illusion of some kind. Know that your boss didn't do this *to you*, he or she just did it. That cuts the charge of the situation in half. Now, take a breath and ask yourself, *What is the level of truth here? Does this accusation have any basis in reality? Does it have any merit or meaning?*

Instead of exploding or becoming defensive, let your practice on the cushion or yoga mat kick in. Breathe in, tune in, ask for guidance and strength from your higher power, and listen *objectively*. Treat your boss and yourself with compassion. Pray for the willingness and guidance to see the situation in a new light. You might consider adopting the attitude suggested in the "How It Works" chapter of the Big Book:

> When a person offended we said to ourselves, "This is a sick man. How can I be helpful to him? God save me from being angry. Thy will be done." We avoid retaliation or argument. We wouldn't treat sick people that way. If we do, we destroy our chance of being helpful. We cannot be helpful to all people, but at least God will show us how to take a kindly and tolerant view of each and every one.

If this is the first time your boss has reacted this way, you might lean toward listening and learning from the experience, even if you feel the person came at you in the wrong way. Whatever the communication might have lacked, you can still work to rectify the problem.

If the person is rude or angry, you might ask them to tone down their voice or, at a later time, let them know how you expect to be spoken to. But you do not want to lash out at work, which might jeopardize your livelihood. It is best to process your feelings later at a Twelve Step meeting or with a good friend, sponsor, family member, or mate. Run the situation by them. Ask for feedback. Process your feelings. Take time to figure out whether your performance was being judged accurately, even if your boss might have lacked the skill to communicate it in a constructive manner. Discern whether he or she was being unfair and coming at you from dysfunction or anger, which is entirely possible. Is this someone you can *never* please?

If this is the case, you have two choices: you can accept your work situation or start to change who *you* are and how *you* react to the world around you. You can be thankful for the opportunity to step back and look at the bigger picture. How are your relationships at work? Is this a place where you feel heard? Is there something you can communicate to your boss and coworkers to shift the energy of your office, even if this takes courage? Can you educate the people around you?

Perhaps, after careful consideration, you are convinced the situation is hopeless. If this is the case, you can take steps to find new work. Rarely do people have the tools to look deeply enough at their situation, to act early, to pause, breathe, and to ask the right questions. But you know how to find space between each breath and each moment. You can approach difficult situations on your own terms without having to handle fallout from fiery tempers and hurt feelings. You can change your situation consciously and with purpose.

No matter what you choose to do, the key to serenity is accepting the situation as it is, not as you would like it to be. Only then can you turn inward to make informed choices and proceed in the right direction—without selling out your authenticity or losing your values.

Mindfulness Works

I know that mindfulness works. I have been at this long enough to know that the equanimity that prayer and meditation have fostered in me leads to positive and unexpected change. Today, some of the very same people who fought me every step of the way ten years ago have said, "I guess you were right."

Integrative medicine centers now exist in hospitals all over the world, and my own Inner Harmony Wellness Centers, which operated in the red for many years, are showing profits. Judges have sought out my programs, and the Pennsylvania prison system even gave me a Volunteer of the Year award, acknowledging the profound shifts my programs promoted in the population they serve.

And my school meditation program was a resounding success as well, with teachers in several Scranton, Pennsylvania, elementary schools teaching meditation to third, fourth, and fifth graders. Soon, these young students were practicing mindfulness meditation for fifteen minutes every day.

The program was such a success that the U.S. Department of Education awarded us a second grant that let us expand the program to include an entire school for a full year. This school offered students meditation sessions for five minutes every morning and fifteen minutes every afternoon.

The University of Scranton conducted studies of our elementary school program and identified quantifiable improvements in grades, test scores, attention, attitude, and behavior. Even the most skeptical parents and teachers found it hard to deny the changes in their children. Some parents reported that their kids had begun using meditation techniques outside the classroom to cope with difficult emotions or even to relax before bedtime.

Needless to say, I have drawn endless inspiration from experiences like these. I have learned, through my spiritual practice, that compassion, tolerance, and perseverance are my strongest tools in the face of doubt and cynicism.

The Promises

The lesson I take from the Dalai Lama and Thich Nhat Hanh, and the lesson I share with you, is that we are all human and with that comes the full range of emotions of which we are capable. At the same time, if we are committed to conscious living we learn how to look at our lives and the world in a new way. We learn to take responsibility for our actions and to come to any situation with compassion and understanding.

When you practice prayer and meditation in your daily life, this understanding and compassion grows exponentially. Soon, you start to realize that the gifts that AA and other Twelve Step programs offer in their "Promises" (from AA's Big Book, pp. 83–84) are real:

We are going to know a new freedom and a new happiness. We will not regret the past nor wish to shut the door on it. We will comprehend the word serenity and we will know peace. No matter how far down the scale we have gone, we will see how our experience can benefit others. That feeling of uselessness and self-pity will disappear. We will lose interest in selfish things and gain interest in our fellows. Self-seeking will slip away. Our whole attitude and outlook upon life will change. Fear of people and of economic insecurity will leave us. We will intuitively know how to handle situations which used to baffle us. We will suddenly realize that God is doing for us what we could not do for ourselves.

Are these extravagant promises? We think not. They are being fulfilled among us—sometimes quickly, sometimes slowly. They will always materialize if we work for them.

These "Promises" stress that "our whole attitude and outlook upon life will change." Nowhere do they say life itself will change. The Dalai Lama and Thich Nhat Hanh both know that life has very real challenges, that the world can be a difficult, and at times, hostile place. But their message is that we can achieve inner peace and serenity, regardless of what happens around us.

If you have a spiritual practice to turn to, a foundation of strength and wisdom from which to operate, then you do "intuitively know how to handle situations which used to baffle [you]." You understand how to face life's ups and downs.

INNER HARMONY EXERCISE

What Would _____ Do?

I often think about the Dalai Lama and Thich Nhat Hanh when I'm in a difficult or stressful situation. I ask myself how these men might approach the challenge at hand. Is there a great leader or teacher you admire, someone who reflects a sane, balanced attitude? When you feel unsure what to do next in a given situation, try imagining how that person might handle it.

What you need: An autobiography, biography, or article by or about a well-known leader or teacher you admire or respect; a pen, a journal, and a timer.

What to do: Spend ten minutes reading the book or article you've chosen—any section will do. Close your eyes and think about the person for thirty seconds.

Now, think of a troublesome situation in your life—one that requires action. For fifteen minutes, without stopping, write down what you think this person would do in the same situation. Would they talk it through with someone? Ask for help? Gather information? Apologize? How would they handle any emotions that came up?

Take a deep breath and read what you have written. You don't have to do what you wrote down, just use it as information. Next, ask your higher power for direction on this issue, and be willing to let go of your own ideas. Complete a five-minute Wheel Meditation (see Chapter 8) and wait to see if you receive any guidance or insight on the matter.

7

My Journey Through the Twelve Steps

At fifteen, life had taught me undeniably
that surrender, in its place, was as honorable as
resistance, especially if one had no choice.

—Maya Angelou

BEFORE I WALKED INTO my first AA meeting, before I had ever heard of the Twelve Steps, or Bill W., or recovery, I believed I was destined to do what my friends and I had always done: drink, do drugs, crash at night, then get up and do it all over again. That was my life and that was my future.

My spiritual awakening began the day I realized that change was even possible. I would listen to the men and women in AA talk about where they had been, where they were, and where they hoped to go; I heard them use words like *acceptance* and *surrender,* and when they would encourage me to stay on my path, I began to believe that I, too, could move toward a brighter future.

Soon, I understood that the Steps were the engine of this change. During the ninety meetings I attended in the ninety days after I left rehab, I would glance up at the Twelve Steps posted on the wall as they were recited aloud. Their meaning would sink in a bit more each time. Slowly, I came around to believing that surrender was something positive rather than a shameful weakness to be overcome. I learned that acceptance wasn't about giving up, but the key to freedom from having to be right all the time.

The Twelve Steps were my liberation. They offered me compassionate and loving discipline, something I desperately needed after living without any meaningful direction or purpose. The suggestion that I seek guidance from a higher power *as I understood Him* made the path even more welcoming. The Steps gave me a wide berth to explore spirituality on my own terms, to move beyond sobriety into a life worth living.

I needed to follow the Steps closely and do what people in AA suggested. I needed that guidance because I knew that, left to my own devices, I would manipulate the system, find a side door, and be back on my downward slide into hell.

We've talked about the Eleventh Step in depth, dissected its deeper meaning, and learned some techniques for practicing it. We've examined how the Step embodies all the other Steps, and heard about the profound shifts prayer and meditation can bring about.

Now, let's look briefly at all the Steps. Be clear that this is not how I think you should or ought to practice them. Instead—just as I might do at a meeting—I am sharing here how I have come to understand the Steps in my own recovery. Glean from it what you will.

You will notice that my relationship with the Steps has moved past my need to cope with cravings for drugs and alcohol to a deeper level, to my need to heal the relationship between my soul and my higher power. It is in this light that I give you my view of the Steps using the Inner Harmony approach.

The First Step

We admitted we were powerless over alcohol— that our lives had become unmanageable.

As my anniversary chips piled up in AA, I was filled with gratitude for the gift of sobriety. Through a regular practice of prayer and meditation, it also become clear that my powerlessness over drugs and alcohol extended far beyond physical symptoms of craving, into my addiction to *chasing*. I chased after happiness, approval, joy, and love that were lacking in my life.

I was powerless to stop believing happiness was outside myself. No one could convince me that peace of mind lay anywhere but in people, places, and things. So strong was this belief that despite all evidence to the contrary, I kept on chasing a sense of fulfillment—but I kept looking in all the wrong places, and used drugs and alcohol to mask the misery that wouldn't go away.

Substances, relationships, cars, and clothes gave me a momentary boost that simulated something like a connection to a higher power. But deep down, it was all a fraud. I had become a feel-good junkie, powerless to stop looking for my next fix.

In rehab, I got my first taste of what it meant to connect with a higher power, with consciousness within. I saw my first glimmer of the truth—that I had created my own monsters, that I had been living life in a house of cards. Sobriety began when I admitted powerlessness over drugs and alcohol, but *recovery* started when I admitted that I was powerless to stop my deluded thinking and behavior. I simply could not let go of my old ideas.

The Second Step
Came to believe that a Power greater than ourselves could restore us to sanity.

When I started on the Second Step, my sponsor introduced me to a new definition of insanity: Doing the same thing over and over and expecting different results. That was how I had lived. Over and over again, I would package my image, amass money and belongings, then wonder why my outsized lifestyle never produced happiness.

Time and again, I was certain each new thing would me bring joy. Sometimes it did . . . for a minute, but never long enough to stop the pain raging inside me. Still, no matter how many times my search for happiness proved fruitless, I clung to the idea that all the answers lay outside me.

I was like a novice swimmer gripping the side of a pool, sure I could never swim without the life preserver of my carefully crafted façade. The idea of floating comfortably as my authentic self was unimaginable. But then, a district attorney's order that I enter rehab or go to prison shattered that façade. It cracked and crumbled into dust. This was how I came to believe in a power greater than myself, how I got my first glimpse of what it might mean to be sane. The ideas that had ruled my life not only ceased to serve me, they were killing me.

Once I acknowledged this truth, I could start looking for a source of sanity. The dark night of my soul led me to the world of inner transformation. I began by observing the changes and growth in the people in rehab and at meetings. Then, as I turned inward, I shifted into another state of consciousness—I felt my inner source and I came home. It was there that I knowingly and innately came to believe that sanity lay in a power greater and wiser than myself.

The Third Step

Made a decision to turn our will and our lives over to the care of God as we understood Him.

I came to understand, through meetings, sponsors, therapists, and most obviously through daily sitting meditation, that I had been suffering from a split between my higher power and myself for most of my life. This was the root cause of my addiction. As I meditated and connected with the divine, as I grew closer to my source with each passing day, I began to trust that if I let go I would be led in the right direction and that my life might unfold in new and positive ways.

This was a major development. For the first time, I stopped looking outside myself for validation, acceptance, and joy because I was regularly experiencing these things within. The more I was able to let go, the more I could surrender to meetings and the path of the Twelve Steps, the clearer I saw that my source was greater than anything I had ever imagined.

My whole life had been about control, but now I had a foundation of trust that let me move safely into unknown dimensions, where I could face my true identity, seemingly for the first time. I became more truthful, more transparent and honest with myself and others. I lived authentically.

The Fourth Step
Made a searching and fearless moral inventory of ourselves.

I took this Step in my third year of sobriety. As I wrote about and recounted all the things I had done to myself and others, the self-image that I had so painstakingly crafted began to melt away. I was in a meditative state, partnering with God as the details of my life spilled out onto the page.

As I witnessed this flow of words, I couldn't help but recognize the ingrained, recurring patterns of dishonesty and fear that had dominated my existence. I could see how I hid behind pride. I began to own my guilt and shame about who I had been and what I had done. I saw how the resentments I was clinging to were false and that the front I presented to the people I genuinely loved had held me captive. I could also see that I had been enmeshed in an insidious pattern of self-pity and victimhood.

I had been told to write my Fourth Step without judgment, and because I had already learned nonjudgmental awareness through meditation, I could step back and recognize that the person who had done all of the things I was writing about was not the real me. Yes, I was responsible for my actions, but it became clear that beneath the layers of my bravado, bluster, and misrepresentation was my pure being.

The Fifth Step

Admitted to God, to ourselves, and to another human being the exact nature of our wrongs.

Doing a Fifth Step with my sponsor was one of the most powerful acts of surrender I had ever known. It was frightening, but sharing my truth with him was the beginning of my commitment to honesty, integrity, and authenticity—a commitment that would change me forever.

This was perhaps the first time I had been totally honest with another human being, looked them in the eye, and presented myself with no embellishments or falsehoods. It was a lesson in unconditional love. I could see God working through another human being and that my connection to divinity did not have to be limited to moments of deep meditation.

When I was done, I experienced an incredible rush of energy. I realized how exhausting it had been to generate and maintain all those lies. I felt lighter than a feather and wept.

The Sixth Step

Were entirely ready to have God remove all these defects of character.

Through the first five Steps, I had admitted my powerlessness, forged a strong connection with a God of my understanding, and dealt with the guilt and shame of my past. I had self-esteem, and my fears had all but disappeared.

By then I had studied with the great Thich Nhat Hanh and dedicated my life to fourteen precepts that included right action, right living, right relationship, right communication, and right speech. I had given up dishonesty with myself and others. When I was being less than genuine, it really bothered me, and I would quickly try to right my wrongs. I could no longer live the old way. I was present, conscious, and ready to have my defects removed.

The Seventh Step

Humbly asked Him to remove our shortcomings.

Before AA, I had to be right 100 percent of the time. I had to be the boss. I had to call all the shots, make all the decisions.

Asking a higher power to remove my shortcomings was the ultimate admission that I did not have all the answers. It was humility in action.

I was becoming free of my ego. The more I surrendered into prayer and meditation, the more I became willing to trust in a divine connection and ask that I be transformed. I wanted my shortcomings to be lifted so that I might become my highest self and do the highest good of which I was capable.

The Eighth Step

Made a list of all persons we had harmed,
and became willing to make
amends to them all.

This tool of transformation brought up yet another round of feelings. When I owned my part in destroying or damaging relationships, I felt more guilt, shame, and fear. But as I wrote out my list and contemplated my motives, I could see that I had been acting out of ego and fear.

Understanding the truth behind my actions gave me the strength and willingness to make amends to the people I had harmed. I was no longer the same person, so there was nothing to fear. It was a chance to connect with the people I cared about in a new way. It was a way to approach them, not looking for forgiveness, but to apologize for any hurt or pain I had caused and ask for the opportunity to rectify the past.

The Ninth Step

Made direct amends to such people wherever possible,
except when to do so would injure them or others.

Making amends to friends, family, and business associates required even more humility and surrender. Much to my surprise, the process was positive. I was met with love and acceptance, and with a sense that we were united with God. What was also surprising, even disconcerting, was that some people would not accept my apology, downplaying what had transpired between us or insisting there had been no wrong. There were times that I even had to argue that I was making the amends for *me*.

What I came to see was that in some cases, the wrongdoing had been in my mind. Nevertheless, the experience had been real to me, and being able to move past it was profoundly healing.

The Tenth Step

Continued to take personal inventory and when
we were wrong promptly admitted it.

I used to practice this Step every day, very consciously. I would hit my knees at bedtime and check in: *Did I harm anyone today? Did I do anything wrong? Did I screw up? Was I dishonest?* I would ask my higher power for strength and guidance in righting any wrongs, in clearing up resentments, and removing ideas or fears that might prevent me from seeing situations clearly. I probably took the idea of inventory-taking too far. I would apologize to people all the time; some of them would laugh at me for being too honest, too hard on myself.

But my early dedication to the Tenth Step changed me. What I've come to realize is that taking personal inventory has become an integral part of who I am. It is how I process thoughts, actions, and circumstances. When I am uncomfortable or out of sorts, I check in. I don't have to do it all at the end of the day. I do it all day long, reflexively, sometimes minute by minute, hour by hour.

The Eleventh Step

Sought through prayer and meditation to improve our conscious contact with God, as we understood Him, praying only for knowledge of His will for us and the power to carry that out.

Through the Eleventh Step I can actualize God all day long. I can live in unconditional love, stop choosing for or against. Through the Eleventh Step I can, in any moment, merge with my higher power.

The Twelfth Step

Having had a spiritual awakening as the result of these Steps, we tried to carry this message to alcoholics, and to practice these principles in all our affairs.

Experiencing union between myself and my higher power opened the doorway to my spiritual awakening. Meetings became my spiritual community. I was able to offer my heart and knowledge to newcomers. The more I operated on a spiritual plane, the more I was filled with bliss and the more I had to give away. The more I gave away, the more I received. This is the ultimate goal of spirituality. When we recognize that there is no God independent of us or our fellow man and woman, we are filled with love, kindness, and compassion. From this point, a life of service is inevitable.

At most Twelve Step meetings, the group leader concludes with the statement, "take what you like and leave the rest." The inference is that no one there is an expert on how you should embrace the Steps or move forward in your recovery. My journey through the Twelve Steps is just that, my journey. Perhaps you can find common threads between my story and your own. Maybe you can find strength and encouragement in my interpretation of the Steps, and draw inspiration from the liberation they offered me from the self-righteousness and certainty that nearly killed me. Reflect on the lessons I shared here, and as we all delve deeper into the meaning and gifts of the Twelve Steps *take what you like, and leave the rest.*

READER/CUSTOMER CARE SURVEY

We care about your opinions! Please take a moment to fill out our online Reader Survey at **http://survey.hcibooks.com**.

As a **"THANK YOU"** you will receive a **VALUABLE INSTANT COUPON** towards future book purchases as well as a **SPECIAL GIFT** available only online! Or, you may mail this card back to us.

(PLEASE PRINT IN ALL CAPS)

First Name _____ MI. _____ Last Name _____

Address _____ City _____

State _____ Zip _____ Email _____

1. Gender
- ❑ Female ❑ Male

2. Age
- ❑ 8 or younger
- ❑ 9-12   ❑ 13-16
- ❑ 17-20 ❑ 21-30
- ❑ 31+

3. Did you receive this book as a gift?
- ❑ Yes   ❑ No

4. Annual Household Income
- ❑ under $25,000
- ❑ $25,000 - $34,999
- ❑ $35,000 - $49,999
- ❑ $50,000 - $74,999
- ❑ over $75,000

5. What are the ages of the children living in your house?
- ❑ 0 - 14   ❑ 15+

6. Marital Status
- ❑ Single
- ❑ Married
- ❑ Divorced
- ❑ Widowed

7. How did you find out about the book?
(please choose one)
- ❑ Recommendation
- ❑ Store Display
- ❑ Online
- ❑ Catalog/Mailing
- ❑ Interview/Review

8. Where do you usually buy books?
(please choose one)
- ❑ Bookstore
- ❑ Online
- ❑ Book Club/Mail Order
- ❑ Price Club (Sam's Club, Costco's, etc.)
- ❑ Retail Store (Target, Wal-Mart, etc.)

9. What subject do you enjoy reading about the most?
(please choose one)
- ❑ Parenting/Family
- ❑ Relationships
- ❑ Recovery/Addictions
- ❑ Health/Nutrition
- ❑ Christianity
- ❑ Spirituality/Inspiration
- ❑ Business Self-help
- ❑ Women's Issues
- ❑ Sports

10. What attracts you most to a book?
(please choose one)
- ❑ Title
- ❑ Cover Design
- ❑ Author
- ❑ Content

TAPE IN MIDDLE; DO NOT STAPLE

FOLD HERE

Comments

INNER HARMONY EXERCISE

The First Time I Read the Steps

The first time I read the Steps I felt relief. I was relieved that I could let go of trying to control my addiction. I was relieved that I could stop trying to control everything in my life and the people around me. I was relieved that I could finally rely on a higher power. What did you feel the first time you read the Steps? How do you feel about them now?

What you need: A copy of the Twelve Steps (see page 252), your journal, and a pen.

What to do: Read all Twelve Steps, then, going Step-by-Step, write down what you felt the first time you read them. Think back to where you were, what time of day it was. Did you read the steps from a poster at a meeting? On the Internet? Did someone give you literature? Did you read the Steps in this book? If you can't remember the first time you were introduced to the Steps, don't worry about it; just think about your general reaction to them early on in your recovery.

When you are done. Read over what you have written. Has the meaning you originally assigned each Step changed at all? Deepened? If you have gone through some or all of the Steps, done a lot of work on them, can you see their gifts at work in your life? This exercise helps you take stock of your progress and shows you that a spiritual journey brings new lessons all the time.

Practice the Wheel Meditation (see pages 207–209) for five minutes to absorb the work you've done.

8

STARTING THE
ELEVENTH STEP—NOW!

We are not cured of alcoholism.
What we really have is a daily reprieve contingent on
the maintenance of our spiritual condition.

—*Alcoholics Anonymous* (the Big Book)

FOR MOST OF MY LIFE, I was sure my problems were *your* fault. I was taught to fixate on externals, so naturally it followed that my happiness depended on outside situations and circumstances. I thought, *If only the people, places, and things around me would change then I could finally be okay.*

I remember that as my one-year anniversary in AA approached, I attended a meeting and listened to people share about problems with spouses, bosses, cars, kids, houses, dogs, cats, you name it. I kept thinking I should raise my hand because it had been weeks since I'd spoken in the group. But then it occurred to me . . . I had nothing to say. I was actually okay. More than okay.

For the first time in my life, I was at peace. I didn't want to hash out the details of my life because I finally understood—really understood—that my problems were an illusion. Prayer and meditation had shown me a new reality. I knew who I was and where I fit in the world. I was far less concerned about what other people did *to* me or *for* me, than I was about how I could be of service in the world.

"One day at a time," that most well-known of all Twelve Step program slogans, serves as both an encouragement and an admonition to those of us in recovery. It reminds us that we only need concern ourselves with staying sober or abstinent for one day. But at the same time, the words warn us that any reprieve we have from our addiction might only last one day.

Anyone who attends Twelve Step meetings for any length of time hears stories about people with decades of sobriety or abstinence who relapse only to find themselves worse off than when they first entered the program. I have seen this firsthand and in the most unlikely of people. One of my own beloved counselors suffered a relapse. As sad as this was, it reminded me that sobriety is a gift given to us each day. I saw how easy it is to get caught up in the things of this world and forget who we really are. So, I practice the Eleventh Step daily because I never know who or what might throw me off balance.

The sooner and more consistently you practice the Eleventh Step, the faster you learn the truth of who you are and the sooner you know your purpose in the world. Prayer and meditation help you feel whole, and this gives you an unshakeable foundation for handling life without using substances or resorting to destructive behavior. Because sobriety and abstinence come to us a day at a time, practicing the Eleventh Step is as important in the first twenty-eight days of recovery as it is in the first year, the first five years, and decades into our sobriety or abstinence.

Some members of Twelve Step programs and some professionals in the recovery community will argue that the Steps should be taken in order. They feel that addicts in the early stages of sobriety or abstinence must stick to the first three Steps because they aren't ready to handle the feelings and emotions that arise when they practice Step Eleven.

I wholeheartedly disagree. If you look closely at the Eleventh Step, it is actually the first three Steps in action. When you pray to understand your higher power's will for you and ask for the power to carry out that will, you are admitting your powerlessness (Step One); you are believing in a power greater than yourself (Step Two); and you are turning your will and life over to a God of your understanding (Step Three).

The Eleventh Step is also considered one of the so-called *maintenance steps*—which include Step Ten ("Continued to take personal inventory . . .") and Step Twelve ("Having had a spiritual awakening . . ."). These maintenance steps, practiced together, are transformative tools that can be worked into recovery at any time. They reinforce the gifts of the program on a daily basis.

To bring home the importance of practicing the Eleventh Step, wherever you are in your journey out of addiction, I have asked several professionals in the addiction field to discuss the value of prayer and meditation at various stages of recovery. All told, they have treated and taught tens of thousands of people for addictions of all kinds.

I begin this section, however, with reflections from one woman who has experienced long-term abstinence in Overeaters Anonymous (OA). She credits much of her success in the program to her ongoing commitment to the Eleventh Step.

A Spiritual 180

 Betsy,* fifty-six years old, has twenty-six years of abstinence from compulsive overeating and bulimia in OA. She prays and meditates every morning.

Prayer and meditation put me in constant contact with God on a daily basis. It's important to understand that it's one day at a time, that there is no carryover from the day before. That's why it is very rare that I miss my morning meditation and prayer.

When I started in OA, I came to meetings for a while then left . . . and let me tell you that was one horrendous year of bingeing and purging. Even though I came back I was still on the fence. I would think, this is really great *except for that God stuff.* But what became clear to me was that the people who had what I wanted had a relationship with their higher power. They had

*not her real name.

long-term abstinence and a certain ease moving through the world. They weren't hanging onto the sides of their chairs.

I remember saying to myself, *if I'm going to have what they have I better get me a relationship with a higher power, too.* Really, that's the point of the program; it is an understanding that abstinence is a gift from God—just in the same way drunks don't get themselves sober.

I was fortunate to have taken a Transcendental Meditation™ class before I ever came to OA, so it was a tool in my arsenal. I'd just never really used it. Today, my daily routine starts with twenty minutes of meditation then prayer. I do it kind of backwards because I think my prayers are clearer after I quiet my mind. I say the first three Steps and then the Third Step prayer [see page 202].

I learned to do this when I lived in California and attended meetings there. It seemed hokey at first, but then I realized how important it was to recommit on a daily basis, to turn my will and life over to the care of God. When I do this, the desire to eat compulsively is gone. God is the "X" in the equation.

I don't always feel anything one way or another when I meditate—sometimes I do, sometimes I don't. Sometimes the experience is very satisfying, sometimes not. But if I don't pray and meditate on a daily basis the cumulative effect is that I lose the feeling that my life is flowing smoothly. I liken it to a musician practicing the piano. He or she doesn't just sit down and play beautifully. They have to practice and do scales. Similarly, a sense of serenity and connectedness doesn't just come upon you.

I often speak about the Eleventh Step at meetings and I will joke that it's unlikely you're going to be "struck serene" in the middle of your day. You have to practice on a daily basis to be in the flow. I suggest that people work prayer and meditation into their daily routines. I tell them, "You can go for six months without brushing your teeth, but why would you?" I know that if I start my day in a peaceful state of mind then I carry that feeling with me throughout the day. I don't bounce around like a pinball.

I also tell people that prayer and meditation are about aligning with God's will and asking for the power to carry it out. Soon, something amazing happens. You do a spiritual 180. You start saying "How can I be of service to the world? How can I best do God's will?"

How do I know prayer and meditation work? It's actually more about what I *don't* feel than what I *do*. I can really sense something is off if I don't do my practice in the morning. Later in the afternoon something just feels really screwy. In fact, I still remember something my TM teacher told us. She said meditation is not "doing nothing." It's like a slingshot at rest. It has all this latent energy in the band, but when you gather it back, when you call on it, it lets you sail through the day. I've always thought that was a great analogy.

A Dimension Filled with Hope

 Juan Lesende, M.S., is Vice President of Clinical Oversight at Treatment Solutions Network in Ft. Lauderdale, Florida. The group refers patients to rehabilitation facilities and monitors their care. A psychotherapist with more than twenty years' experience in addiction treatment, Lesende says his passion for his work stems from his background in the Human Potential Movement, which explores connections between spirituality, science, and mental health.

Over the course of twenty years, I have worked with populations of between fifty to sixty individuals who rotate in and out of
the rehabilitation facilities where I've worked every thirty to forty-
five days: that's thousands of people. When we introduce a
spiritual practice like prayer and meditation into treatment,
especially in the first days of sobriety, those who embrace it
have the most success staying clean and sober without relaps-
ing. I say this from very personal experience that I stand by
100 percent. I have observed it, not just in one person, but
as a definite pattern.

Twelve Step programs are spiritual at their very core. Prayer
and meditation are a gateway into that spirituality. Once
patients have an insight into this "waking up" and this way of
living, when they see spiritual principles applied, then they
experience the benefits. And it's not only that they become
clean and sober, they become new people. The founder of AA
and the Twelve Steps talked about having a "spiritual awakening." In other words, sobriety is not about going from being an
addict to not being an addict. It's about becoming a new
human being with new aspirations and hopes.

When patients practice prayer and meditation from the start,
it moves them into a dimension filled with hope. The hope comes
from learning that there is something available to them that they
can do, something that soothes them. They learn that they can
move away from drugs or alcohol without being totally helpless,
alone, and without recourse. It motivates them to say, "I am
going to embrace this treatment and a new way of life. I can
live without depending on drugs or alcohol." I think this kind of
hope is essential for recovery, and my observation is backed up
by a lot of research.

Also, in my experience, treatment centers that incorporate meditation, yoga, tai chi, qigong, or other spiritually-based practices into treatment have fewer incidents of people leaving against medical advice. And they report fewer conflicts among the patients and with staff. After treatment, the patients who incorporate these practices into their lives do better. If they do relapse, they are more likely to ask for help, return to treatment, and get back into recovery.

The first ninety days and first year in recovery are usually very difficult. People need to reestablish broken relationships and broken careers, often working at jobs they would have found demeaning before. I've seen that those who embrace a spiritual practice find meaning in what they're doing. Instead of feeling displaced or ashamed, they are able to view their work as a practice of being humble, of learning simplicity—all part of practicing a spiritual path. As a consequence, they come through the year without feeling desperate or depressed; they make it through a very hard time.

Those with long-term sobriety—if they continue in the program and continue to pray and meditate—go through life in a new way. They become peaceful; they can handle struggles. Problems are still there, but they can face them with a certain grace and serenity. They also become sponsors, gaining the ability to be of service without being preachy or arrogant. They taste the positive effects that prayer and meditation have on their emotional and psychic health. I'm speaking about the best outcomes, of course, but I have seen them so often. When people in recovery stick to a spiritual practice, whatever they engage in—relationships, work, service—they are usually successful at it.

In fact, I still have close ties with people I knew when I started as a mental health tech twenty years ago; the ones who continued their spiritual practice are successful by any definition you can think of. They have become successful parents, husbands, wives, employees, friends, mentors, and lovers. The frequency with which this happens indicates that it cannot be a coincidence. These are the people who adopted this spiritual way of thinking or believing, and usually it started in the first days of treatment.

Breaking the Ego

 Nicholas Colangelo, Ph.D., is CEO of Clearbrook Treatment Centers near Wilkes Barre, Pennsylvania. I taught meditation there for several years. The facilities include a sixty-six bed adult center and a forty-seven bed adolescent center. A licensed drug and alcohol counselor, Colangelo has worked at Clearbrook for twenty years.

When you're talking about the Eleventh Step, there are two very separate things going on—prayer and meditation.

Prayer *breaks* the ego by connecting us to the unknown and to godliness, which is important for the alcoholic or addict who thinks he knows everything and that he's God-like. I know this first-hand because I've been sober for thirty-five years. I also know that meditation brings us back to the essence of who we are. It lets us visualize all that we are supposed to become.

Prayer is important because if we walk around thinking, *I'm it,* then meditation isn't really going to do anything for us. If I'm an egomaniac sitting in a seminar or yoga class, I'll be the guy making fun of everyone and being a pain in the neck because it's all about me. That's why we tell people, "You're all walking around like little gods, and how's that working out for you? You're in a rehab, not at Big Sur."

Prayer lets us become humble. When we try to overcome addiction on our own, we're fighting as if we actually have the power to do it. Whatever our drug of choice, we try to control it and make adjustments. Prayer helps us identify something outside ourselves; it breaks that type of behavior and those kinds of thought processes.

When people come in, we talk to them about prayer immediately. We explain that prayer is being quiet and still and asking to understand what our maker wants us to be or do each day. It's certainly not a petition to God. Prayer is the doorway through which meditation can affect us.

Meditation can be tricky early on, especially if someone feels guilty, remorseful, or ashamed of their addiction and transgressions; they might run into a horror show and it can be scary. They haven't cleared away the wreckage of their past and made peace with it yet. This is especially true for people with trauma issues like physical and sexual abuse. Also, today, more than ever before, we see more young people—kids who think they can jump over tall buildings. They have broken every moral code—stealing from parents, all kinds of things—and there is tremendous hurt, pain, and unrecognized guilt. Put them into meditation and they can run into dragons.

We don't want them to run away from meditation, so we introduce it carefully. If you prepare someone—and that's the job of a good treatment center—meditation is a very powerful thing. We let them know what might happen when they meditate, and we don't move too quickly. Our meditations are very basic. We begin by helping them relax, to go to a peaceful place. We explain that the more we pray and meditate, the more we become ready to look deeper. We can learn to manage outside stressors by having a safe house inside us.

We ask everyone to try meditation, but we don't force anyone to participate. Some won't because they don't like the concept of finding a higher power, or they've grown up with religious training they don't like. But we try to make it something they can digest. We keep it simple. We don't use a gong or get too ritualistic because some people rail against it.

Meditation is eye-opening. It moves emotional boulders out of our way. I think of addicts as blocked straws. When they meditate, the air goes through them. They become a clear channel and an empty vessel. I know that when I meditate I can connect with the possibility of my goodness and my godliness. Meditation connects who I am now to who I was when I was born.

Addicts clutter up their lives with shame and secrets. We tell them it's important to start dealing with these secrets right away. (Secrets become the boulders.) Prayer and meditation move them out of the way, and then everything starts to shift. We can't help but look deeper into ourselves—at our mind, body, spirit, at diet and exercise.

In my own life, meditation got me through my earliest days of recovery. I was a typical wreck in a treatment center. I was ashamed and broken. So many things bothered me. The goblins—*Who is going to pay the bills? I lost the house. My wife is divorcing me.* But for the first time, I was able to go to a quiet place and experience peace.

What was most important was that I learned there was a

direct alternative to the peace I got from my drug of choice. For so many addicts, this is the first time they have any idea that there's another way to find peace of mind. Most addicts would tell you that they would trade anything for peace of mind. They just want an escape from the crazy thinking and the torment of being *sick and tired of being sick and tired.*

Meditation helps us understand that by being powerless and doing what we are told to do in recovery, we actually *get* the power to live and experience life differently. This is true for alcoholics, gamblers, sex addicts, or food addicts. Ultimately, there is only one desperate need in every human being, and that is to be loved and to be able to love. If we do all the Steps, and if we practice prayer and meditation, we have a better chance of experiencing it.

Where Is Your Attention?

Lee McCormick is founder and owner of the Ranch, a healing center in Nunnelly, Tennessee, that treats people struggling with substance addiction, eating disorders, behavioral addictions, trauma, and other issues. He is the founder of Spirit Recovery, which offers consciousness-oriented travel, workshops, and conferences, and he's my partner in the Integrative Life Center, a new outpatient treatment center in Nashville.

The biggest issue anyone deals with coming into recovery is his or her foundational beliefs. They're taught that their beliefs define who they are. At the Ranch, we work with them to change their core belief system, which is inherited from family, culture, and the world. We help them create a relationship with *themselves.*

Beliefs come from where we put our attention. Prayer and meditation—the Eleventh Step—is a gateway to understanding that our core beliefs might not be real, that life is really a mystery, that there's a whole lot more to being human than we'll ever know. There is not a person on this planet who really knows what it means to be human, so why not give the divine the respect it deserves?

My programs take a creative approach to meditation that does not require clients to sit straight on a cushion in the lotus position. Prayer and meditation require being as still as you're capable of being, but "still" is relative—it might be one thing for you, another for me. That's why the prayer and meditation we offer is only limited by our creativity. For example, we offer sweat lodges, open-eye meditations, and walking meditations.

The sweat lodge is a sacred space. There is a fire, hot rocks, and ceremony involved. It's a tradition that is spiritually and physically engaging. Sitting with the fire, sitting with those stones, talking about how pouring water over the rocks brings up the steam that makes us sweat. That is a form of meditation. We talk about all the aspects of life represented in the rituals of the sweat lodge.

I also take people down to the river for an open-eye meditation. We sit and watch the water. We look at every aspect of creation as alive, aware, and conscious. When people in recovery watch the water move, things begin to move in them. Emotions happen, thoughts happen. The river is a great metaphor for the life that moves through us continually. Because of the way our mind has been trained to operate, we are usually not in the flow of life. We're in the thought *about* what's going on. We get hooked into our opinions, beliefs, and stories. When we pay attention to beliefs and thoughts, we're not in the moment.

I also take people on walking meditations through the woods and ask them over and over again, "Where's your attention?" Are they thinking about getting back home? Getting high? Or are they experiencing where they are?

When I do this with them often enough they start to get it. They realize for the first time that their attention is all over the place. It's the beginning of awakening, of becoming aware of what they do, of recognizing how they choose to direct their attention in any moment. This allows them to practice directing their attention, and it's the foundation for taking responsibility. This is a very big deal for them, because if they don't learn to take responsibility, life can run over them.

Prayer and meditation are the groundwork for recovery. Clients begin to witness how they function as a human being. Some people realize that their whole life is nothing but a story, that they've been living in reaction to stories they keep telling themselves. Some people actually shut down when this happens, because they are terrified to think they might be responsible for a huge aspect of their own suffering. It's overwhelming to realize *it's been me doing it to me,* and at the same moment there's a tremendous opportunity because they finally realize they can stop what they've been doing. They can change.

I Was Really There

Meredith Hardee, M.S., L.P.C., and Debbie Rappa-Webb both work on the front lines at two rehabilitation centers in Pennsylvania. Hardee has been a spiritual counselor at the Caron treatment centers in Wernersville for nine years. Rappa-Webb has been a specialist at the Marworth treatment center in Waverly for six years. Both introduced formal prayer and meditation programs into their facilities.

Meredith Hardee: The first thing I explain to everyone who comes in is that they need to have some sort of Eleventh Step happening. I tell them that Bill Wilson, the founder of AA, got sober, not because of his values, but through a spiritual awakening. He hit his knees and he hit the Eleventh Step.

It doesn't take a rocket science for them to get that if the founder of AA couldn't get sober without a spiritual awakening, neither can they. I always encourage them to read about Bill Wilson and the vision that led him to create AA.

Another thing I share about is that there are a lot of ways to pray and meditate: running, swimming, listening to a thunderstorm, doing the rosary. It gives patients the freedom to find their own way to connect with a higher power rather than just on bended knee the way Bill Wilson did.

And there are people who just can't sit still. If they're in detox and have been using heroin and speed, there's just no way in early recovery we're going to get them to slow down. I had a woman who prayed in the shower because it was the only place she could feel connected to her source.

Since most people in their first thirty-one days of recovery can't sit in silence without getting anxious, I use guided imagery to give them a taste of what it means to focus and quiet the mind. Then, when they're in extended care or they head out after thirty, sixty, or ninety days, their meditation begins to change. It can be less guided and take on a more Buddhist perspective of moving the mind inward. At this level, the meditations I present become more calculated and tailored for the population I teach.

To start, I often create a beach scene because it's someplace they've been. They can see the sun and the rolling waves, feel their feet sinking into the sand. It's something their brains and bodies remember; it taps into them on a cellular and psychic level. I show them they can meet their higher power on the beach.

People often tell me, "I was really there." Meditation expands consciousness beyond the physical body. Some people who come in addicted to pain medications say it is the first drug-free relief they've had from pain.

For extended-care patients who have been in treatment sixty to ninety days, I might lead a meditation in which they imagine jumping off a mountain. They feel themselves spinning in the dark then landing safely. I use this to help them understand Steps One, Two, and Three. I use meditation so they can experience the Steps and the feeling of letting go on a deeper level.

I believe patients have to get Steps One through Three down—admit powerlessness and make that connection—but I weave in the Eleventh Step from the start. When people experience prayer and meditation, some of them for the first time, there's a surrender, an acceptance, and a complete sense of peace. Whether or not they are able to sustain it when they leave, they've at least had a meditative experience; it's in their bodies.

Sometimes they're afraid they'll lose the experience, but I tell them, "You can always sit down, take a few breaths, remember the day we meditated together, see yourself in the circle, see the people around you, and that memory is going to come back." For the people who really get it, it will seep into their soul.

Debbie Rappa-Webb: A lot of the patients come to my workshops because they're having trouble sleeping; some even joke that they've come to take a nap. But once they're there, I talk about prayer and meditation. I explain they don't have to wait to start the Eleventh Step, because without a higher power connection they're not going to be restored to sanity. I tell them that on their individual strength alone there's not much hope for them. They can easily fail.

We start with guided relaxation to put them into a meditative state of mind. Some of them are full of anxiety; others are in physical pain. Without drugs or alcohol, their nerves are on the outside of their skin. They focus on their breath, and it relaxes their bodies. The meditation takes them to a really peaceful place.

Some actually do fall asleep, because they're on heavy medication. But for most of them, it helps them relax and reduces stress, cravings, and anxiety. It's a big change because they're used to having a drug do that for them. And even if they don't connect in the spiritual sense, it's a start. Because if they're tight and tense it's going to be difficult for them to connect with a higher power.

From there we practice mindfulness, getting still, stepping back, and noticing. Noticing where their emotions are. Are they tense? Fearful? I go on to explain that prayer is communicating, asking questions of our higher power, and that meditation is being still and listening. A lot of times, we pray for guidance, but we can't hear the answers until we get quiet and still. Once someone gets relaxed, and they have the openness and willingness to connect with a power greater than themselves, then emotions come up. The truth reveals itself.

At Marworth, we always encourage patients to work on the Eleventh Step and the other maintenance steps every day. This helps them keep their sobriety. They can look over their day, clear up resentments and anything else that happened, and get themselves right. We tell them this is something they're going to need to do on a daily basis. It's going to make life a lot easier when they get home. It provides structure.

When I see patients begin to make that spiritual connection it's beautiful. So many of them come in feeling guilty and ashamed; they don't feel worthy of connecting to a higher power. A lot of them are surprised by the experience. It's totally new to them. They're addicts and alcoholics—where would they have had the chance to experience this kind of thing? A lot of them cry; I see them wiping their faces. Even those with a spiritual upbringing and belief in a God struggle with their spirituality because of what's happened in their lives. The meditation helps them through that process. The guided imagery is like taking them through a prayer.

Calling Them to Come Away

Joyce Walker retired two years ago as the mental health coordinator for a medium-security correctional facility in Pennsylvania, where she worked for ten years. She attended my Inner Harmony Workshop, then asked me to develop a meditation program for the inmates at her prison.

I asked Peter to teach at our Special Needs Unit where most of the men were drug abusers who were also physically and mentally challenged. They were between the ages of nineteen and sixty. At first, no one took the meditation classes very seriously; in fact, some people I worked with thought it was crazy. "You're teaching them what?" they'd ask.

We are talking about a really tough bunch: sex offenders, robbers, you name it. They took a lot of ridicule for coming to Peter's classes, but they really looked forward to those days because Peter taught them how to cope with the difficult stuff that went down in there. These are guys who could get themselves into a state on any day. Meditation would help calm them down.

We'd have eighteen to twenty guys in the classes at any time. Peter would explain to them, "Meditation will help you not pick up." He also told them his story so they really understood where he had been. He was sincere about what had happened in his life, so they related. Because Peter was from the outside, he could be more personal with the inmates than any of us who worked there. Usually, these were guys you simply could not trust. They were very manipulative, but Peter knew how to work with them.

It was a voluntary program, but we always had very good attendance. That's how we knew it was really touching people. They enjoyed it; they felt at peace by going there. In fact, you could see them calm right down when those meditation bells would go off. It was almost like it was calling them to come away, to find an inner peace. It's a wonderful and important thing when someone can learn that.

I used to sit in on the classes. My coworkers would warn me,

"You'd better watch it in there." Yes, I always had to be alert, and we always had guards watching, but I could relax a little bit. You would see the men calm right down. Peter taught them that skill.

There was one guy I remember in particular. He used to get picked on terribly. I think he would have gone off the deep end were it not for Peter's classes and the meditation CDs and CD players Peter donated. That guy used them all the time.

After the program ended, I learned the training and continued teaching the classes. Eventually some of the inmates helped me teach through a peer assistance program. One guy was fantastic with visualizations. He could put you in a trance. Peter had taught him well.

Peter genuinely cared about these guys and they really respected him for that. He never gave up on them and neither did I. We both shared that philosophy. Not giving up on them is not easy. But to give you an idea of the impact the workshops had, there's a plaque on the wall with Peter's name on it. He was Volunteer of the Year.

I know that only a small percent of these guys succeed, but that's what was so important about this program; meditation could be the one thing that changed someone's life.

The people who contributed to this chapter were chosen because their collective wisdom about addiction is invaluable. It is my hope that their reflections on the Eleventh Step inspire you to start the Eleventh Step, no matter where you are in your recovery. *Now* is the time to commit to a regular practice, whether you are a beginner, a veteran, are in danger of a relapse, or have sought help again after a new bout with your addiction.

If you start the Eleventh Step now, for a few minutes a day, whether or not you think you can find the time, focus, or energy to pray and meditate, you will not be disappointed. Adding prayer and meditation to your recovery works. If you already dedicate time to attending meetings, going to therapy, making phone calls, and reading literature—this is one more investment of time that will pay off in spades. You will gain a deeper understanding of who you are. Not only will this understanding make you feel centered and strong, it will propel your recovery to a new level.

INNER HARMONY EXERCISE

Eleventh Step Detective

If you've spent years struggling with addiction, you know what it feels like to be lonely and isolated. In recovery, we quickly learn that our survival depends on our ability to let other people in—to learn from them, to hear about their successes and mistakes. Using this newfound openness, try to reach out to other people in recovery to learn as much as you can about how they practice and perceive the Eleventh Step. Become an Eleventh Step detective.

What you need: Your journal, a pen, and the willingness to reach out for help.

What to do: Devote the coming week to gathering information about the Eleventh Step. Talk to friends in recovery, your sponsor, your therapist, a spiritual leader, anyone who knows anything on the subject. Ask them about their experience with prayer and meditation.

If they are in recovery, find out if they pray and meditate daily. If so, what does their practice look like? What time of day do they pray and meditate and where? Do they have an altar or do they sit in a park? How long do they meditate? What do they say about receiving guidance from a higher power? Does it happen for them at all? If it does, does knowledge of their higher power's will come in the form of intuition? Or do they find answers by reaching out to others for help? If you are seeing a therapist ask what he or she thinks about prayer and meditation. If you follow a particular religious faith or spiritual practice, talk to a clergyman or advisor.

Bring your journal with you as you conduct your interviews so you can write down anything interesting you learn and any questions that might come up. Not everyone will have something positive to say, but try not to judge the answers you hear or compare your practice to theirs. There is no right or wrong here, you are just staying open to new thoughts and ideas that might help you in your own practice. Your higher power often speaks to you through other people. Listen and see if your detective work yields any gems of wisdom.

9

PRAYER AND MEDITATION IN OTHER FORMS

*When your mind unconditionally embraces
what your body is feeling—when your thoughts,
feelings, actions are moving as one—you merge
into the integrative experience of yoga.*

—Yogi Amrit Desai

IN CHAPTER 5, YOU LEARNED HOW to connect to yourself and your higher power by paying careful attention to the breath. Now, let's expand your understanding of meditation by exploring practices that are more physically engaging: yoga, breath work, sound work, and walking meditation. All are excellent alternatives to sitting meditation if you have trouble staying still or just want to mix up your daily routine.

Yoga

A half century ago most people in western society viewed yoga as a mysterious and exotic practice for health nuts, hippies, or Indians in loincloths. But as the twenty-first century dawned, interest in health and fitness exploded and most people could recognize yoga's long list of physical and mental benefits.

Yoga improves muscle tone, flexibility, strength, stability, stamina, concentration, and circulation. It reduces fat, stress, and tension; lowers blood pressure; stimulates the immune system; and alleviates symptoms of diabetes, heart disease, arthritis, asthma, back pain, carpal tunnel syndrome, chronic fatigue, depression, anxiety, epilepsy, and headaches. Most obviously, yoga's gentle, flowing postures and controlled breathing techniques help foster a sense of well-being and calm.

Today, yoga studios are found in cities and small towns alike, with classes offered at gyms, community centers, and even nursing homes. Despite yoga's wild popularity, most people still think of it *only* as a physical workout that aids in flexibility and relaxation.

Yoga is far more. *Yoga* is an ancient Sanskrit word meaning *unity* or *oneness*. In its purest sense, yoga is a way of life designed to develop consciousness and lead to spiritual enlightenment. Yoga originated in India about five thousand years ago. It was conceived as an alternative to the Vedic religion, which stressed symbolic ritual rather than direct spiritual experience. Yoga asks us to remain aware throughout the day—aware of the way we move, eat, breathe, and interact with people and our environment. Yogic postures and breathing techniques are practices associated with this lifestyle.

Certainly, you can practice yoga for its physicality and still glean some of its spiritual benefits. But for our spiritual growth and recovery from addiction—we *intentionally* practice postures (*asanas*) and breathing techniques (*pranayama*) to learn about ourselves and connect to our higher power. We practice yoga *on purpose* to unite body, mind, and spirit.

Inner Harmony Yoga

Inner Harmony Yoga begins with *intention*. Drawing from Hatha, Raja, and Bhakti yoga, and linked to the lineage of my teacher Yogi Amrit Desai and his teacher Swami Kripalvananda, Inner Harmony Yoga asks you to set a clear intention to reconnect with your spirit.

As someone in recovery, you can use yoga to rediscover the part of you that never drank, used drugs, acted out, and so on. Yoga can give you an awareness of who you are and how you react. As in sitting meditation, yoga postures and breathing techniques can help you cultivate a sense of tranquility so you move past thought and ego to an experience of your higher power's wisdom. It is in this spirit that I recommend my students begin their practice with this ancient Hindu prayer:

Lead me from the unreal to the real.
Lead me from darkness to light.
Lead me from time-bound consciousness to the timeless state
*   of being.*

Life On and Off the Mat

In this prayer, we state our intention to bring the lessons learned from our practice *on* the mat into our lives *off* the mat. How does this work? How can yoga postures and breathing techniques teach you about life?

When you execute a posture you often ask your body to move beyond what your mind thinks it can do. When you hold a pose, sensation builds. You can begin by setting an intention to notice how this feels and how you respond. When the physical going gets tough, do you want to give up? Or do you push, seek some goal, strive to strengthen a particular part of your body? Are you kind to yourself or harsh and critical? Does your ego kick in? Do you really let go?

Notice any subtle layers of tension, holding, or limitations in your body. Take a breath and move deeper into the pose, letting go just a little bit more. Check in and see how your mind reacts. Are you resistant to trying something new? Are you irritated? Elated? Defeated?

If you can observe sensation and emotion as they arise when you're on the yoga mat, you can observe them when you're caught in traffic, waiting in line at the grocery store, or dealing with a difficult person. You can use what you learn about yourself in a yoga posture to choose how you react in any given situation. A deep breath can slow down your thoughts and your need to react during an emotionally intense situation, just as breathing into a posture can help you stay with physical intensity.

The more attuned you become to your breath and your body during your yoga practice, the more familiar you become with the way energy or *prana* flows through you, through your relationships, your work, and more. This *engaged consciousness* helps you discover who you are, how you show up in the world, and how you can change.

Prana

Before we discuss the mechanics of postures and breathing techniques, it is important to understand *prana,* a Sanskrit word meaning *primary energy*. Prana is sometimes translated as *breath* or *vital force*.

The universe is a manifestation of prana, which is the power by which all things and beings in the universe are created, thrive, are destroyed, and are created again. Prana expresses itself in cycles and rhythms, in light waves, heartbeats, the ebb and flow of oceans, and the movement of planets around stars. Yogis believe that God can be realized and directly experienced through an ability to understand, use, and direct prana. This is why we honor prana in our yoga practice.

Yoga teaches us that we experience prana as waves of energy and sensation. Our goal is ride these waves by being present and paying attention to our world of sensation. Inner Harmony Yoga uses this inward focus and meditative awareness to harness prana's innate healing power. Energy follows awareness. Therefore, wherever you put your focus, prana will flow.

The first tool we use to connect with prana is conscious breathing. We use full yogic breaths, or diaphragmatic breathing. When you direct your attention to the breath you become attuned to energy and movement and the idea of things arising and passing away. You become aware of constant change. The prana flow exercise that follows uses the breath to familiarize you with the nature of prana.

Prana Flow Exercise

Take a deep breath. Stand at the front of a yoga mat with feet planted and arms raised. This is the Mountain pose (more about this later). Use the stillness of the posture to notice any subtle

Prana Flow Exercise

movements in your body. Feel the rise and fall of your breath. Is it rapid or slow? Deep or shallow? Pay attention to the moment of stillness between each inhalation and exhalation.

Next, notice the larger sensations of the body. Feel your leg muscles engaged and experience the effort it takes to keep your shoulders and arms lifted toward the sky. Feel energy move through you as you hold the pose and your muscles tire. Turn your attention to the feeling of air on your skin, the quiet pulsing of blood in your veins. Let the sensations direct your awareness as you continue to press your feet into the mat and reach your hands to the sky. Feel the dynamic stillness as the life force courses through you. Continue holding the pose, but only use the muscles you need. Breathe deeply as you relax your belly, neck, and back.

Has your mind kicked in? Do you find yourself thinking, *How much longer can I hold this? I'm tired. I can't do this.* Or do you fixate on sensations? *My triceps feel hot; my shoulders feel sore . . .* relax the mind. Try to refocus on the breath, staying conscious. Breathing in and out. Trust that you are safe, that the sensation of prana builds then flows like a river.

Continue to stay still, but tune into the energy you feel moving through your body. Remember, energy follows attention; you can amplify and direct prana by shifting your inner focus. If the sensation gets too intense, soften the flow by shifting your attention to other parts of your body. Resist the urge to shift around or release the pose. Let go into the sensation and stillness.

Ease out of the pose and slowly begin to move. Feel how the sensations change. Let your body integrate this new feeling and move as it wants to. Does a stretch feel good? Bending at the waist? Your body will tell you what it wants to do. Follow prana's wisdom.

Yoga Postures (*Asanas*)

In the Prana Flow, you just observed how holding a posture can generate intense sensation. *Asana* actually means "staying" or "abiding" in Sanskrit. Because of this intensity, it is important to use precision and care in your practice, being sure to listen to your body as you proceed. If you are pregnant, recovering from surgery, have a chronic illness, or have *any* questions or doubts about whether or how you should practice yoga, please consult a physician. For safety, it is best to use a yoga mat. As in sitting meditation, be sure to carve out adequate time and space for your practice, with plenty of room to move safely and freely.

Working Your Edge

When we practice yoga we encounter our personal *edge,* the point at which physical and mental limitations keep us from moving deeper into a pose. We don't judge this edge; we breathe into it and merge with the intensity of the experience, keeping our chest and heart open. Then, gently, we take a small and safe step beyond our comfort zone into the unknown. We direct our attention and awareness into the sensation of the pose. This awakens prana at all levels of our being—mental, physical, emotional, and spiritual.

The real measure of your practice is whether, little by little, you can identify these physical and mental edges and move *slightly* beyond them each time. This takes courage. Courage isn't about being fearless or pushing yourself too far. It is about being willing to experience your fear, limitations, and old patterns, and slowly move beyond your expectations *without harming yourself*. As you stretch your body and mind, your courage will grow.

Soon you will discover an increasing sense of lightness and curiosity; you will move toward a more open and genuine practice. This stretching is a metaphor for the way you live. Once you recognize your ability to move out of your physical comfort zone, you begin to see it in action in your life, as you move through your days.

It is important that you approach your yoga practice with patience and acceptance. Don't expect perfection; just do your best to keep your attention focused on correct alignment. This prevents injury and maximizes benefits. If you find yourself going offtrack, don't be critical. Notice this, make a correction, and gently continue your work. Strive to become a witness, an observer, rather than a judge.

Please note that it is more important to use proper form in a pose than it is to move deeper into it. You will find your edge within the physical limits of proper form, not by going around it.

Press Points and Energetic Extensions

Extending energy through opposing press points creates proper form. Imagine holding a piece of string with one end in each hand. To create a straight line, simply pull the ends of the string in opposite directions. Press points work the same way. To bring part of your body into correct alignment, simply press the ends of that part in opposite directions. For example, if you want to straighten your spine while in a sitting position, press your sitz bones down and lift the crown of the head up. The energetic extension of any pose is in the area *between* the press points. This is where you want to stretch and where prana flows through a pose.

Mountain Pose (*Tadasana*)

Mountain Pose

TECHNIQUE: Stand with your feet together and palms pressed against one another in the prayer position.

Press down into the feet and extend up through the crown of the head. Inhale, extending the arms overhead as you continue pressing the palms together. Drop the tailbone and tighten the buttocks and inner thighs as you press into your feet. Feel the extension up through the spine and out the fingers. Press your arms against your head and slightly back. Relax the shoulders and take deep breaths. Gaze straight ahead, keeping your chin parallel to the floor.

Release the pose slowly, maintaining the prayer position as you lower your arms and drop them to your sides. Close your eyes, take a deep breath, and feel the relaxation.

PRESS POINTS: Feet, palms, and arms.

ENERGETIC EXTENSION: from the feet to the hands and fingers.

COMMENTARY: Keeping the arms close to the head and slightly back opens the lungs to energy. Extending upward opens the abdominal organs and energizes the spine. Strong leg and buttock muscles align the hips and back, energizing the pelvis. This pose also grounds the mind and opens all the energy pathways in the body. It activates and stimulates the organs, enhancing circulation, digestion, respiration, elimination, reproduction, and menstruation. It also helps correct posture problems.

Half Moon Into Standing Back Bend

(Ardha Chandrasana into Anuvitasana)

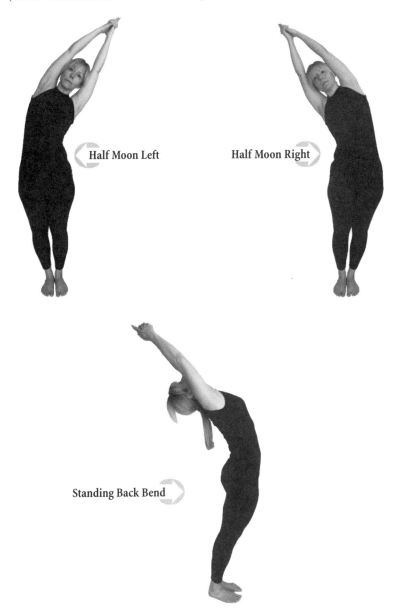

Half Moon Left

Half Moon Right

Standing Back Bend

TECHNIQUE: With hands in prayer position and feet together, stand tall and look straight ahead. Inhale, extending your arms straight overhead and pressing your palms together. Interlace your fingers in temple position. Drop the tailbone while you firm up the buttocks and inner thighs by pressing into your feet. Hold this while you extend up through the spine and index fingers. Press the arms to the head so they are positioned just behind the ears.

Next, press the hip to the right as your upper body extends to the left. Breathe. Keep shoulders and hips square. Press into your right foot. Extend up through the right side of the body and out through the fingers, eyes looking straight forward.

Come back to the center by pressing both feet into the floor, inhaling as you return. Keep breathing as you extend through the fingers and bring your arms overhead. Repeat on the other side.

Moving into Standing Back Bend (Anuvitasana), drop the tailbone as you tighten the buttocks and inner thighs. Then press down into the feet while extending the chest upward. By extending out through the fingers and pressing the hips forward, you will create a back bend. Be sure to keep the crown of the head aligned with the spine. Continue to breathe fully as you hold the position.

As you release, inhale, press into your feet, and slowly come up. As you exhale, you will release your hands and extend your arms forward to shoulder height—palms should face each other and remain shoulder width apart.

PRESS POINTS: Feet (left foot on right tilt, right foot on left tilt), arms, palms.

ENERGETIC EXTENSION: Each side of the body from the feet up through the fingertips.

COMMENTARY: As you hold, do not twist or turn. Try to maximize the energetic opening by keeping palms together, arms close to your head, and by extending. Keep contracting the buttocks and leg muscles, bringing the hips slightly forward into proper alignment while you protect your back and energize your pelvis.

The Half Moon pose opens each side of your body. It is especially beneficial for digestion and helps warm the entire body. By alternating the extension on each side, you give the spine a lateral stretch, which keeps it flexible and supple. This benefits the nervous system. The arm position helps break up tension in the neck and upper back. It also opens the lungs.

The back bend allows contraction of the kidneys. When you release the posture, the kidneys are flushed with blood. This increases circulation. The back bend also helps you open and stretch the abdominal organs as you strengthen your lower back.

Forward Bend (*Pada Hastasana*)

TECHNIQUE: Begin by bending your knees and extending the torso forward and down. Place your chest on your thighs, or as close as you can get. Place your palms on your calves and slide your hands down so you can hold your ankles. Try to ease your elbows and forearms toward each other. Also, try to ease your forehead toward your knees. Continue to breathe. As you exhale, press into your feet and extend your tailbone toward the ceiling. Be sure to straighten the legs only to the point at which your belly

Forward Bend—Full Posture   **Forward Bend—Modified**

remains touching your thighs. Do not force the stretch. Continue to breathe as you maintain the pose.

PRESS POINTS: Feet, crown of the head, and elbows.

ENERGETIC EXTENSION: From the heels to the crown of the head, including the backs of the legs through the spine and neck.

COMMENTARY: If you cannot get your fingertips underneath your heels, hold the back of your ankles. If you are overweight and can't breathe or move easily into the bend, separate your feet and keep your knees bent for the Modified Forward Bend.

Keep your eyes open and press into the feet. This helps to maintain balance. Do not force the posture. This pose helps create a deep opening for the spine and back muscles. It releases tensions deep in your neck and shoulders. Compressing your abdominal organs stimulates your intestines, stomach, gall bladder, liver, and spleen. When you invert, it reverses the blood flow in the upper torso, which stimulates glands and lymphatic flow. This posture also helps calm the nervous system.

Integration (*Vajrasana*)

Integration—Vajrasana

TECHNIQUE: Begin by sitting on your heels. Rest your palms on your thighs, sit up straight, and extend through the crown of the head. Keep your shoulders down and back, your heart center/chest open. As you close your eyes, relax deeply. Give into this state of calm.

COMMENTARY: This pose will help give your body, mind, and spirit a brief rest. It allows you to integrate the work you have done.

Cobra (*Bhujangasana*)

TECHNIQUE: Lie on your stomach. Keep your forehead and palms on the floor and align your fingertips with your shoulders. Press your elbows in and back. Keep extending through the toes as you press your feet together and downward. Keep pressing your

Cobra

pelvis into the floor. Push your palms into the floor with your fingers actively extended. Inhale as you lift your forehead, chin, and chest until you reach your navel. Pull your elbows back and extend your chest forward from the heart. Keep breathing fully as you hold the pose. Continue extending through the crown of your head as you keep it in line with your spine. Stretch back through your toes, forward through your heart, and out through the crown of your head. This activates the entire body. Breathe in and out as you hold. Exhale fully, then release. Turn your head to one side and relax your arms at your sides. Continue to relax and breathe deeply.

PRESS POINTS: Pelvis, chest, feet.

ENERGETIC EXTENSION: Through the feet and up through the crown of the head.

COMMENTARY: Try not to execute the movement with your hands. Use your back muscles to lift and lower yourself. Your hands merely support your weight. This pose is meant to strengthen your lower and middle back while increasing spinal flexibility. It also strengthens the nervous system and stimulates the adrenal glands and abdominal and pelvic organs. It energizes the lungs and heart, facilitates increased blood flow to the kidneys, and aids thyroid functioning.

Boat (*Navasana*)

TECHNIQUE: Lie on your stomach with your forehead down and tops of your feet flat on the floor. Keep your arms forty-five degrees away from your body and your palms down. Bring your feet together, but separated slightly. Then, press your pelvis into the floor as you inhale and lift your legs, upper body, and arms simultaneously. Keep extending back through the toes, forward through the heart, and out through your fingers. Keep breathing as you hold the pose. With each inhale, lift up higher. Release and exhale fully, then turn your head to one side.

PRESS POINTS: Hips and pelvis.

ENERGETIC EXTENSION: Extension through the toes, crown of the head, and the fingers.

COMMENTARY: The goal is to practice this posture consistently and without strain. There is a difference between working hard and straining your muscles. Doing more, but holding the posture for shorter increments builds your strength and raises your energy level. This posture helps strengthen all your back muscles, energizes reproductive organs, increases the flexibility of your spine, and, finally, allows new blood flow to the kidneys and adrenal glands.

Child Pose (*Garbhasana*)

Child Pose

TECHNIQUE: Get on your hands and knees then slowly sit back on your heels. Exhale. Lower your forehead until it rests on the floor. Place your arms at your sides with your palms facing up, then stretch them out in front of you with your palms facing down; or, you may stack your hands under your forehead. Continue to breathe into the upper back and relax.

To release, gradually bring your body back up into a sitting position.

PRESS POINTS: Hips and forehead.

ENERGETIC EXTENSION: Forehead through the tailbone.

COMMENTARY: This gentle posture requires more letting go than effort. Do not tense any muscles. This position is a very good counterpose to the back-bending postures. It serves to relax and open your back muscles, spine, and hips. It also provides a gentle massage to the abdominal organs.

Corpse Pose (*Shavasana*)

Corpse Pose

TECHNIQUE: Lie on your back and separate your feet slightly wider than your hips. Keep your arms at your sides with the palms turned up. With eyes closed, take a full, deep breath, and let go completely. Allow every part of your body to relax: toes, feet, legs, hips, back, hands, arms, shoulders, neck, and face. Your body should feel as if it is melting into the floor. Continue to release any tension you are holding.

COMMENTARY: Complete relaxation in Shavasana lets the wisdom of prana in the body make the adjustments it requires after asana practice.

Yoga Sequences

The following are sequences you can incorporate into your daily practice, which we will discuss in detail in Chapter 10. I suggest beginning any spiritual practice with the Complete Yogic Breath.

Complete Yogic Breath with Movement

This sequence is used to coordinate the breath with three movements. It is comprised of three inhalations through the nose followed by a forceful exhalation through the mouth as you move your arms.

TECHNIQUE:

1. Stand straight with your feet hip-width apart. As you press down into your feet, extend up through your torso and the crown of your head. Keep looking straight ahead with your arms at your sides. Breathe in one-third of the way. Extend your arms out in front of you with your palms facing together.

2. Now, inhale two-thirds of the way and extend your arms out to shoulder height.

3. With a final inhalation, raise your arms overhead, keeping them shoulder width apart.

4. As you exhale forcefully, swing your arms down to your side, bend your knees, and fully expel the breath from your lungs.

Repeat this for seven full breaths.

COMMENTARY: Moving your arms opens the chest and enables deeper breathing. Using your diaphragm helps your lungs work at full capacity. Coordinating your breath with body movement increases circulation, warms up your body, and readies it for yoga postures.

This pose keeps your movements flowing and coordinated with your breath while you remain focused. The breath should be

Complete Yogic Breath with Movement

vigorous, with full inhalations and forceful exhalations. Pull your abdomen in as you complete each exhalation. This empties your lungs and allows for even deeper inhalation.

The power of rhythm, combined with body movement and breath, helps clear the mind of extraneous and disruptive thoughts. This readies you to enter any spiritual practice with a balanced body, steady mind, and open heart.

Sun Salutation (*Surya Namaskar*)

The Sun Salutation is a series of complementary poses and a staple of most yoga practices. We use it to continue to open and warm up the body following the Complete Yogic Breath. One can tell by the name that the sun salutation is a great sequence to do first thing in the morning.

TECHNIQUE:

1. Keep your hands in prayer position with your feet together. Press your feet down while pressing the crown of the head up. Keep looking straight ahead.

2. Inhale. Extend your arms straight overhead and gaze at your hands. Drop your tailbone, contracting your legs through the buttocks and inner thighs. Press down into your feet while extending the chest upward. Maintain the extension through your fingers and press your hips forward. This will create a slight back bend.

3. Exhale. Bring your hands into the prayer position. Fold downward as you look at your fingers. Bend at the knees; place your hands on the floor, thumbs next to your little toes. Press your forehead toward your knees.

4. Inhale. Step backwards with your right foot into the Lunge position. Keep your right toes curled under. Press your right heel back while keeping your front knee directly over your ankle. Lift your chest and look up.

5. Hold your breath. Step your left foot backward into the Plank position. Make sure your body remains straight with your shoulders directly over your wrists.

6. Exhale. Bring your knees to the floor; extend your tailbone upward as you lower your chest and chin toward the floor. Keep your elbows in—sternum between the thumbs.

7. Inhale as you press into your palms and slide your chest forward and up into Upward Dog as you simultaneously lower your pelvis. With your knees on the floor and elbows slightly bent, pull the elbows in and back. Be sure to extend upward through the spine and out through the crown of the head.

8. Exhale, then press your hips back and your tailbone up into Downward Dog. As you extend through your arms, press your palms into the floor and press back your hips.

9. Inhale. Step forward with the right foot into a Lunge. Lift your chest and look up.

10. Exhale. Step forward with the left foot into a forward bend. Keep your feet together. Ease your forehead and chest toward the legs. Extend the tailbone up in the direction of the ceiling.

11. Inhale. With your palms together, rise up slowly, looking at your
    hands as you extend your arms straight overhead. Drop your tail-
    bone and squeeze the buttocks and inner thighs. Press down into
    your feet and extend the chest upward. The extension carries out
    through the fingers as you press your hips forward to create a
    slight back bend.
12. Exhale. Lower your arms and return to standing prayer position.

Note: A point to remember—inhale as you open the body and
exhale as you fold the body (whenever you contract the abdomen,
you are exhaling). Always try to develop a rhythm by synchroniz-
ing your movement with your breath.

COMMENTARY: This can be done as a stand-alone exercise and is best repeated up to seven times. **Alternate stepping the right and left legs back into a Lunge.** The Sun Salutation has been called a total body warm-up because it synchronizes movement and breath, creating strength and endurance. This posture activates all your muscle groups and strengthens the body. It also tones, stretches, and invigorates your body while it massages and tones your internal organs.

Basic Yoga Sequence

Combine the above sequences and postures as follows:

1. Complete Yogic Breath with Movement
2. Sun Salutation (two times)
3. Mountain Pose
4. Half Moon
5. Standing Back Bend
6. Forward Bend
7. Integration
8. Cobra
9. Boat
10. Child Pose
11. Integration
12. Corpse Pose

Smiling and Crying on the Mat

When you incorporate yoga into your daily routine, you start to feel good, look better, and become more relaxed. You gain flexibility, energy, grace, and awareness. Soon—perhaps during the deep relaxation of Corpse Pose (*shavasana*)—you might notice a different kind of shift. Your heart cracks open with love or joy, sadness or grief. Yoga can bring up waves of emotion and feelings that have been locked in your body for years.

Allow these feelings to come up; watch with love and compassion. There is no need to judge emotions as good or bad. Try to move your mind into the sensations these feelings evoke. Let go of thoughts and experience your emotion as prana, as a beautiful release of energy. Return to your breath, relax, and feel the sensation. Witness the experience and appreciate the journey you've been brave enough to take.

Breath Work—Pranayama

The Sanskrit word *pranayama* means management and mastery of prana. It is composed of *prana,* which you now know means "breath" or "life force," and *ayama,* meaning "to extend." Conscious use and control of the breath lets you move through deeper and subtler layers of tension both in physical postures and in life. These breathing techniques keep your mind steady, especially when you encounter mental and emotional boundaries including fear, resistance, criticism, and doubt.

Your breath changes noticeably when you face physical, mental, and emotional stress. At these times, most of us hold our breath or breathe erratically. Through pranayama exercises, you can learn how to slow down your breathing, to make it deliberate and rhythmic. This ability to consciously change your breathing patterns is an extraordinary tool that can help you cope with uncomfortable feelings, shift out of old habits, and replace them with new awareness.

Pranayama can be practiced while you execute a pose. As you move in and out of postures, pay attention to your breath, especially at your edge where there is a tendency to hold air in. Witness your breathing pattern. This is the best indicator that you are experiencing fear or doubt about moving deeper into a pose. Try to adjust your breath so it is steady and even.

You can also practice specific techniques that are deeply meditative and strengthen your ability to stay aware of each breath. These techniques include forcing and holding inhalations and exhalations. These practices can be done while you are standing or sitting. However, if you get light-headed, it is important to sit.

Sounding Breath (*Ujjayi*)

Sometimes called Darth Vader or Ocean Breath, this form of pranayama, with its intense sound, is calming and grounds you in the present. You create this sound by gently constricting the throat while you breath—as if you were trying to fog up a mirror or eyeglasses. If you are drowsy, the sound of this breath helps to engage your mind.

Technique:

1. You can sit straight with your spine elongated, or lie down, relaxed, in corpse pose (*Shavasana*).

2. Keep your mouth closed and slowly inhale through your nose while contracting the back of your throat slightly as if making an *ahhh*

sound. This creates a slight hissing sound at the back of your throat as air passes through the windpipe. You can regulate the flow of your breath by constricting the back of the throat to prolong your inhalations and exhalations.

3. As you continue with slow inhalations, your abdomen relaxes and expands as in the complete yogic breath.

4. Continue contracting the back of the throat slightly as if trying to make an *eeee* sound, but with the mouth closed. As you slowly pull the abdomen in and up, exhale and fully empty your lungs. The flow of your breath should be long, slow, and controlled.

5. Continue inhaling and exhaling in this way.

COMMENTARY: This is a focused, grounding technique that combines slow breathing and sound. It brings the mind into the present. It is great for calming anxiety.

Fire Breath/Quick Outward Sniffs (*Kapalabhati*)

This fast, restorative breathing technique is useful when you're bored, losing focus, or falling asleep. *Kapalabhati* brings oxygen quickly into the lungs and brain.

TECHNIQUE: In *Kapalabhati*, exhalations are forced. Inhalations are spontaneous. There is a split second of retention after each exhalation. To begin:

1. Breathe out through the nose; simultaneously push in your abdomen then relax it and allow an inhalation to happen passively. This is one round.

2. Repeat the exhalations steadily and rhythmically with an emphasis on each exhalation.

VARIATION: Instead of using both nostrils, you may alternate closing off the right nostril, then the left nostril.

COMMENTARY: This breathing technique cleanses and purifies the whole respiratory system by forcing air out of the lungs. It clears the mind and improves concentration by increasing oxygen in the system.

Alternate Nostril Breath (*Anulom Viloma*)

This rhythmic, gentle breath work is meditative, calming, and creates a sense of balance.

TECHNIQUE: Inhale through one nostril, retain the breath, and then exhale through the other nostril in a 1:4:2 ratio. As an example, use the count 2:8:4, as described below.

1. Sit in a comfortable position. Bring your hand to your nostrils. You will be using your thumb to close the right nostril and your third and fourth fingers to close the left nostril.

2. Close the right nostril with your thumb, while breathing in through the left nostril to the count of two.

3. Then, hold your breath, closing both of your nostrils to the count of eight.

4. Keep your left nostril closed with your third and fourth fingers. Then, to the count of four, breathe out through the right nostril.

5. Keep your left nostril closed while breathing in through the right nostril to the count of two.

6. Hold your breath with both nostrils closed to the count of eight.

7. Keep your right nostril closed with your thumb, and to the
count of four, breathe out through the left nostril.

The sequence above represents one round of *Anulom Viloma.*

COMMENTARY: *Anulom Viloma* awakens prana, thus creating a balanced flow of energy through the body. It has a calming and balancing effect on the mind.

Spinal Breath

This is a simple exercise that is useful before a sitting meditation or after any of the active breathing practices.

TECHNIQUE:

1. Exhale. Pretend that your breath flows from the top of your head down through the base of your spine.
2. Inhale as if the breath is being carried from the base of the spine up to the top of the head.
3. Repeat exhaling down and inhaling up.
4. Feel that your breath is flowing in a delicate, bubbling river from top to bottom and bottom to top.

COMMENTARY: This exercise can be done while meditating and as part of *Yoga Nidra* (see page 184). To aid relaxation, this is best done lying flat on your back in *Shavasana,* the corpse pose.

Sound Work—
Yoga Nidra and Mantras

Before we talk about Yoga Nidra and mantras, you will need a brief understanding of chakras.

Chakras

Chakra is a Sanskrit word that means *wheel, circle,* or *turning.* In yoga, chakras are physical and spiritual energy centers or vortices located along the center of the body from the base of the spine to the top of the head. There are seven main chakras that correspond to various emotions, characteristics, and energies including light (color) and sound. They are also associated with elements found in nature. In ascending order (with Sanskrit names in parentheses), they are:

1. Base or Root Chakra (*Muladhara*). At the perineum, located between the genitals and anus, this chakra is associated with sexuality, stability, and security. Color: Red. Sound: *Lam.* Element: Earth

2. Sacral Chakra (*Svadisthana*). At the sacrum (small of the back), this chakra is associated with reproduction, creativity, and joy. Color: Orange. Sound: *Vam.* Element: Water.

3. Solar Plexus Chakra (*Manipura*). At the base of the sternum, above the stomach, this chakra is associated with digestion, power, transformation, and spiritual growth. Color: Yellow. Sound: *Ram.* Element: Fire.

4. Heart Chakra (*Anahata*). At the center of the chest, this chakra gov-

erns the heart, circulatory, and respiratory systems. It is associated with love, devotion, and passionate emotions such as jealousy, grief, hatred, and loneliness. Color: Green. Sound: *Yam*. Element: Air.

5. Throat Chakra (*Vishuddha*). Located at the base of the throat, this chakra corresponds to communication, self-expression, independence, clear thought, and security. Color: Blue. Sound: *Ham*. Element: Ether.

6. Brow Chakra (*Ajna*). Also called the third eye, this chakra is located slightly above and between the eyebrows. It is related to spirituality, wisdom, and deep thought, and is the gateway to higher consciousness. Color: Indigo. Sound: *Om*. Element: Light.

7. Crown Chakra (*Sahasrara*). At the top of the head, this chakra relates to thought, intuition, and enlightenment, and is the gateway to the spiritual world. Color: Violet. No associated sound or element.

Yoga Nidra (*Deeper Harmony*)

Yoga Nidra means "yogic sleep." It is a state of deep relaxation, beyond a meditative state, into something that nears sleep. In Yoga Nidra, we remain deeply relaxed but conscious. In this state, we are highly open to the transformative powers of the universe. That is why we enter Yoga Nidra with the intention to grow and change, to become our highest self.

The brain registers four major patterns of brain waves: beta, alpha, theta, and delta. Beta waves occur when we are awake and alert. Alpha waves form when we are relaxed but alert. Theta waves represent a state of drowsiness, and Delta waves form in deep sleep. Yoga Nidra moves us through all four of these brainwave patterns, although we never lose consciousness as we do in sleep.

Yoga Nidra initiates shifts from the deepest core of your being, opening you up to change at a very unconscious level. Through your practice of Yoga Nidra, which we call Deeper Harmony, the voices of your physical, emotional, and spiritual bodies align. Deeper Harmony is one of the most powerful tools for self-discovery, moving you beyond the mind, intellect, and ego, into a direct experience of who you are and who you always were. Deeper Harmony allows the extraordinary powers of your own insight, intuition, inspiration, and creativity to unfold, moving you into a new dimension of being.

PREPARATION FOR YOGA NIDRA:

1. Create a comfortable, safe, and quiet environment with a moderate temperature.
2. Practice a few asanas then refresh yourself by resting in *Shavasana* (corpse pose).
3. Perform seven rounds of *ujjayi* sound breathing as you calm the mind.
4. Chant seven rounds of the sacred word *Aum* or *Om* before dropping into silence.
5. Pray for guidance or find an intention for your practice.
6. Relax and release all effort.

TECHNIQUE:

1. Lie in *Shavasana,* the corpse pose. Your spine will be straight and your feet and arms at a comfortable distance from your sides. It is ideal to place a thin pillow under your head and to use a towel or blanket to keep your body warm. Methodically move your attention through each of the areas below:

   • The forehead and the throat.
   • On the right side of your body: Your shoulder, elbow, wrist, tip of the thumb, tip of the index finger, tip of the middle finger, tip of the ring finger, tip of the little finger, and back to the wrist, elbow, shoulder, and throat.
   • On the left side: the shoulder, elbow, wrist, tip of the thumb, tip of the index finger, tip of the middle finger, tip of the ring finger, tip of the little finger, and back to the wrist, elbow, shoulder, and throat.
   • The space between your breasts (heart center), right breast, heart center, left breast, heart center, navel, lower abdomen.
   • On the right side: hip, knee, ankle, tip of the big toe, tip of the second toe, tip of the middle toe, tip of the fourth toe, tip of the little toe, and back to the ankle, right knee, hip, and lower abdomen.
   • On the left side: hip, knee, ankle, tip of the big toe, tip of the second toe, tip of the middle toe, tip of the fourth toe, tip of the little toe, and back to the ankle, right knee, hip, and lower abdomen.
   • The navel, heart center, throat, and forehead.

2. Spinal Breath (see page 182)

3. Enter into Yoga Nidra through the chakras as follows:

- Focus your attention on the brow chakra. This is the space between and above the eyebrows. Settle in that place for several breaths or for a minute or two.
- Focus your attention on the throat chakra and visualize the moon. Settle in that place for up to two minutes.
- Focus your attention on the space between the breasts, the heart chakra, and allow yourself to be free of any thoughts, sensations, or experiences.
- Just relax deeper into the stillness and silence.
- Stay in that silence and try to give in to the experience. With practice, the period of time might lengthen.
- After a while, thoughts, impressions, or sensations might return. They might arise gradually, or as a sudden jolt. When this happens, it is a sign that your Yoga Nidra session has finished.
- Gradually move your attention outward, moving through the awareness of peacefulness, the awareness of the smooth, relaxed breath, and the stillness of the physical body.
- Bring this silence with you, as you move your fingers and toes. Slowly open your eyes.
- After Yoga Nidra, you can move gently into sitting meditation.

Set an intention to use this experience as a vehicle for transformation. You might even carry the feeling of stillness with you all day long—in everything you do and everywhere you go. Do not judge or analyze whether you succeeded or failed. Your one goal is to return to your intention again and again.

Mantras

Mantras are sacred sounds that are attuned to primordial energies. Through the repetition of these sounds—either aloud or internally—you can align your mind, body, and spirit to powerful cosmic vibrations. A mantra is a specific sound or vibration that helps you sink into quieter, more peaceful levels of consciousness.

The word *mantra* is derived from two Sanskrit words: *manas* or "mind," and *trai*, which means "to free from." We use mantras to free us from the never-ending movement of the mind. When chanted or repeated mentally for long periods, a mantra can connect us to calming energy and expand our awareness. Like other meditative practices, mantras help us move beyond thought so we can perceive the world in new ways.

Bija Mantras

Bija mantras or "seed" mantras are pure, simple sounds that resonate at specific frequencies associated with the chakras. *Om,* also pronounced *aum,* is such a sound, especially the *mmmm* part, which sounds like the buzzing of a bee. Inhale and exhale smoothly and slowly and repeat the *mmmm* sound mentally. *Om* is associated with the brow chakra or third eye, and consists of four distinct sounds. It starts with an *aaaaa*, which you can feel in the solar plexus chakra. As the sound rises into the heart and throat chakras it changes to *uuuu*. Then, as the sound enters the back of the mouth, it changes to *mmmm*, as it passes over the upper palate, and travels out of the body.

The sound *aum* is inherent in all mantras. Its three elements *aa, uu,* and *mmmm,* resonate with waking, dream, and deep dream states. Ultimately, repeating the sound *aum* can pierce the veil of illusion and bring about transformation.

If you have a physical, emotional, or spiritual issue on which you would like to focus, refer to the list of chakra points on pages 183–184 and chant the corresponding sound. For example, if you are experiencing tightness in the pit of your stomach, or if you would like to bring change into your life or cultivate a sense of power and strength, chant the bija mantra *ram* associated with the solar plexus chakra.

You can repeat a mantra for any length of time, from one minute to several hours.

Primordial Sound Meditation

When you practice primordial sound meditation (PSM), you are assigned a personal mantra. You can receive a personal mantra from an Inner Harmony Yoga instructor (see Resources section) or another PSM practitioner. Your silent mantra is calculated using Vedic mathematical formulas based on the time and place of your birth. Reciting this mantra internally helps you move into the space between thoughts, into a state of inner calm and pure awareness that Deepak Chopra calls "the gap."

Primordial sound meditation doesn't force your mind into being quiet; it puts you in touch with a sense of quiet that is already there. Even when your mind is agitated, you always have access to this inner stillness and calm beneath the turbulence of thought and feeling. As your body rests in deep meditation, your mind can still be awake but in calm, restful awareness.

When you become comfortable with your personal mantra and repeat it daily, you merge with its vibration. Just as you might hear a song that you love in your head, you begin hearing your mantra internally and spontaneously throughout the day. The more you repeat the sound, the more it becomes ingrained in your mental pathways. It becomes an ever-present *hum* at the back of your mind.

Whenever you need concentration or a calm, peaceful mind, your mantra is there, available for you to call on. You only need to recite it once or twice internally, and your whole mood and state of mind can shift. It is a river of sound in the depths of your being, there for you to call on as needed.

When you work with a personal mantra, you begin by saying it aloud. As you become absorbed in the sound, it grows quieter spontaneously, until the mind grows calm. You can let go of the vocalization and move the sound inward, into your mind, until you grow calmer and more still, your thoughts slipping away.

A mantra, repeated every morning, can reverberate silently in your mind all day, bringing order and harmony with it. Because the chakras are associated with bija or seed mantras, you can also repeat a mantra to cultivate a feeling or to aid physical healing in that energy center.

When we use mantras, we are no longer at the mercy of the vibrations of other people, places, or things. We generate our own vibration, attuning with our own soul and our higher power, guiding our minds and bodies at the most intimate and fundamental level of our being. When we chant silently or aloud, we attract and generate our own physical and spiritual energy.

Walking Meditation

In walking meditation, we move through space, keenly aware of our surroundings but focused on the sensations in our bodies. In a sense, walking meditation is a beautiful metaphor for the balance we seek as we move through life. If you don't watch where you are going, you might trip and fall. Similarly, if you fail to pay attention to your heart, mind, and body as you go through the day, you can lose your spiritual bearings and fall into emotional turmoil and stress.

Walking meditation is an excellent practice for people who are new to meditation and those who have trouble sitting for any length of time. It is gentle and very easy to practice. It is also useful when you want to break up long sitting meditation sessions, especially if you have achieved a deep meditative state and do not want to disrupt it.

A walking meditation session can be as long as you like, but ideally it lasts from fifteen minutes to an hour. It is best to find a quiet, safe place in nature: the beach, a park, a path through the woods, or along a river. If that is not possible, an indoor track, a gymnasium, or the perimeter of a large room will do. If you live in a city, try to walk when and where you won't be in danger or distracted by cars, bicycles, skateboarders, and so on. You can even use a treadmill if bad weather or crowding does not permit going outside.

TECHNIQUE: Begin with your eyes closed and cultivate a sense of smiling on the inside. Let the warmth of this inner smile fill your being. Take a long deep breath, filling your lungs with air.

Let it out. Stand tall, distributing your weight evenly on both feet. Acknowledge the earth beneath you. Feel it rise to meet you. Remember what a miracle it is that you are standing on an immense, round planet spinning through space.

Now, open your eyes and focus on your senses. If you are in a park, see the trees. Are they a soft green, alive with the first buds of spring? Are they turning a vibrant kaleidoscope of colors in the fall, or are they stark and bare in midwinter? Can you *smell* grass or warm smoke from a nearby chimney? *Feel* the wind against your skin. Is it icy? Humid? Dry and gentle? *Listen* for birds, a train whistle in the distance, or the faint echo of traffic and planes. Open your mouth; does the air have a *taste*? Or do you only notice the remnants of breakfast or toothpaste on your tongue?

Turn your attention inward again, this time keeping your eyes open. Maintain a soft gaze, focusing on nothing in particular. Notice the tiny adjustments of balance it takes just to stand there. Take one more long, deep breath and take your first step, moving slowly. Not unnaturally slow, just a nice comfortable pace. Move your attention to the bottoms of your feet. Notice how they roll across the ground as you move. First one, then the other. Heel, sole, toe; heel, sole, toe. Left, right, left, right. Notice the distance each foot travels as it moves across the ground, lifts, and returns to the ground. Does the soil crunch beneath your shoes? Are you barefoot? Do you feel grass? If you are wearing shoes, feel how they grip your feet. Do they move across the tops of your feet? What do your ankles feel like? Is there tension in them? If there is, breathe into the tension, feel it melt away.

As in any meditation, if your thoughts wander, simply notice them, and gently and kindly bring your attention back to the sensations in your body.

Continue to walk and move your attention to your lower legs. Feel your calves flex and release with each step. Are these muscles tight? Do your pants brush against your shins? Can you feel your socks shifting around your ankles? Move your attention up your leg to your knees. Notice their hingelike quality, the way the lower leg swings from the upper leg. Let go of any tension in your knees. Move your focus to your thighs and feel how the impact of each step reverberates up from the ground, through your feet, shins, knees, and into the powerful thigh muscles.

Again, notice the hingelike quality of your hips, as your thighs, knees, shins, and feet swing from the hips with each step. Breathe, releasing any tension you hold in your hips. Allow gravity to swing your legs forward and back as you take each step.

Next, notice how your lower back and spine connect to your hips; feel the twisting of each vertebra as you walk. Feel your torso rotate on the axis of your spine, moving the front of your body gently back and forth, through your abdomen and rib cage. Put your attention in your chest, as your lungs expand and contract with each breath. Has your breath quickened the longer you've walked or has it slowed down?

Feel how your body's core holds you upright, its power driving your movement through space. Let your attention rise like a helium-filled balloon into your shoulders. Examine your arms, how they swing freely back and forth from your shoulders, alternating with each step, your lower arms swinging from the elbows. Feel the air between your fingers. Is the temperature of the air that hits the front of your hands different from the temperature of the air you feel on your palms?

Now, let your attention travel to your neck. It moves slightly, adjusting with each step to keep your head facing forward. Can you feel your hair moving as you walk, shifting with your movement and the wind? How do your cheeks, jaw, and forehead feel? Is there tension there? Notice the crown of your head. Breathe into any tension you feel, and think of a giant gush of water, flooding your body from the crown of your head, moving through you, and washing out any stress through your toes. Take another deep breath, and as you feel all the parts of your body move in harmony with each step, think of yourself as a mobile, all your parts swinging through the air with each step.

Keep walking, noticing the sense of well-being. Now see if there is a distinct rhythm to your steps. Are you moving to a particular count? Just notice. Do you breathe once for every three steps? Every five steps? Count them for a while. And if you want, change it up, walking and counting a little faster, then slower, returning to a natural comfortable gait.

Play around with your focus, move your mind from your feet to your head and back. Finally, focus on your feet again, noticing all the micromovements it takes to accomplish each step. Every time you set out on a new walking meditation, you can choose which part of your body you'd like to focus on. It keeps the practice fresh and alive.

Bring your walking meditation to an end by coming to a stop. Close your eyes, take a deep breath, and thank your body for taking you on this short but rich walk of awareness. If you practice walking meditation regularly, you will find that it becomes second nature to pay attention to your body. When you walk around a store, around your house, or around your office, your mind will naturally return to this state, noticing the sensation of every step. You will become more attuned to your physical state and more skilled at releasing tension throughout the day.

INNER HARMONY EXERCISE

Meet the Chakras

The chakras are powerful centers in the body, vortices where prana collects and radiates. Focusing your attention on these points can be very healing. Use this exercise to familiarize yourself with your chakras, to learn how to move your attention to these energy centers in times of stress or difficulty.

What you need: this book, a chair, a pen, and your journal.

What to do: Execute three full yogic breaths, then sit comfortably at a table and close your eyes. Take a few more deep breaths. Slowly reread the section on chakras, stopping after you've read about each point. Begin with the root chakra. You are going to focus on qualities, feelings, sounds, and colors associated with each chakra. Does one of these things stand out for you? For example, when you read about the solar plexus chakra, does the word "digestion" resonate for you? The word "power"? Perhaps the color yellow is striking, or you are drawn to the image of fire. Note whatever stands out most in your mind.

Now close your eyes and think about the word, image, or sound, and mentally move it into the chakra. For instance, see the color yellow filling that chakra, radiating out and around it. Breath into the color and any sensation that this evokes.

Repeat this for each chakra. If you want to spend more time on one chakra than another, that is fine. Notice which chakras draw you in and which ones you want to run away from. This might tell you where you need healing and where you can turn for comfort.

When you are done, take a few more deep breaths, and if you want, write about anything you discovered or any emotions you felt.

10

WALKING THE WALK: DAILY PRACTICE

You have it in your power to make your
days on earth a path of flowers
instead of a path of thorns.

—Sri Sathya Sai Baba

W HEN WE ENGAGE IN SELF-DISCOVERY and personal growth, when we live connected to our higher
power, the way we use time begins to shift. Finding time for prayer
and meditation can seem like a chore at first. You worry that you've
got too much to do, that you'll forget something important, or
that you're being self-indulgent. Life's endless chores take priority
and soon the days, weeks, months, and years slip away without
your ever finding time for *you.*

If you make an effort to practice the Eleventh Step each day—
even for a minute or two at first—slowly but surely, direction and

strength arrive. Little by little, you find ways to reorganize your day to accommodate your practice. You *want* to pray and meditate. They become priorities.

A Simple Beginning

Ideally, try to devote thirty minutes or more a day to prayer and meditation (fifteen minutes in the morning and fifteen minutes in the evening). I know from personal experience that this is a highly effective way to move forward in life and recovery. And as a yoga and meditation teacher, this is my recommendation. However, I am also a realist and understand that when it comes to spiritual practice each of us has different interests, tolerances, motivation, and time constraints. The important thing is to make a beginning. Try it. Right now.

Read the instructions in the next few sentences, then close your eyes and follow them. *Take a deep breath. Feel the air filling your lungs all the way. Notice the brief moment of calm after you inhale and before you exhale. Now, let the air out, all the way. As you do, feel tension and stress leaving your body along with the air . . .*

That's it. That is the building block of any meditation. Mindfulness. Awareness. You can do it. A few seconds at a time, one minute at a time.

A Brief Story About Making a Beginning

A forty-nine-year-old woman I know went from being a couch potato to completing two marathons in less than two years. When I asked her how she accomplished this impressive feat, she told me that a friend of hers had introduced her to a running club comprised of two dozen groups ranging from walkers to elite-level runners. The club met weekly, with each group starting at three miles and working their way up to twenty miles over the course of seven months.

She decided to try it, she said, because she was told she could begin at a pace she could tackle without too much effort. From there, she followed weekly routines for her level, including directions on how far and fast to go on any given day. The training, designed by a man who had won the New York City Marathon, was so gradual and well structured, that when race day arrived, she said it was a challenge, but "very doable."

"For the first time in my life I had found an exercise program that met me where I was and moved me forward gradually. I knew that if I followed the plan my body could do more than I ever dreamed possible."

In that spirit, I have outlined several configurations of meditation routines that make the Eleventh Step "very doable" on a daily basis. You are encouraged to dive into the Thirty-Minute Meditation, but if that feels overwhelming, you can begin with something as simple as the *Smiling Meditation,* which takes seconds, or a quick and easy practice I call the *One-Minute Meditator.*

From there you can choose from among sessions that last five minutes to two hours. All of these meditation practices and sequences are outlined in Chapters 7 and 9. Use them as is or combine them to fit your schedule, situation, or frame of mind. You can also consider them a jumping-off point for creating your own routines. You will find some techniques more comfortable than others. Choose what works for you. Whatever options you choose, my hope is they meet you *where you are,* so you can lead a life that is more fulfilling than you ever dreamed possible.

First *Think* in the Morning

Most people wake up, start their day, and still manage to remain unconscious. They get dressed, grab breakfast, and run out the door still half asleep, robotic. But when you are in recovery, when your goal is sobriety, abstinence, and sanity, it is a good idea to pay attention to your thoughts first thing in the morning—right there in bed. As soon as you're aware that you're awake, ask yourself, *what am I thinking?*

Are you happy, cranky? Rested, tired? Don't judge or fight where you are, just notice. This establishes an *intention of awareness* for the day. This is a spiritual touchstone you can return to at any time during the day.

Morning Prayer and Readings

If you have created an altar, this is a good time to move over to it, though it is not necessary. Begin with a prayer. Ask that your thoughts, feelings, and actions for the day be guided by your higher power. If you're dealing with a specific problem or are in the midst of a situation you find challenging, drop an intention into your awareness that you are seeking guidance on this issue.

This is also a powerful time to read (or recite) prayers from your religious tradition or from a daily meditation or self-help book. Many people in Twelve Step programs find guidance and comfort by reciting Steps One through Three first thing in the morning. Or they contemplate the Serenity Prayer (written by theologian Reinhold Niebuhr), which is a staple of most Twelve Steps programs.

Serenity Prayer

God grant me the serenity to accept the things I cannot change;
The courage to change the things I can;
And the wisdom to know the difference.

There are several prayers in the Big Book and AA's *Twelve Steps and Twelve Traditions* from which people in recovery draw direction and inspiration. There is value and wisdom in them whether you are in a Twelve Step program or not.

Third Step Prayer

God, I offer myself to thee to build with me and to do with me as thou wilt. Relieve me of the bondage of self, that I may better do thy will. Take away my difficulties that victory over them may bear witness to those I would help of thy power, thy love and thy way of life. May I do thy will always!

Seventh Step Prayer

My Creator, I am now willing that you should have all of me, good and bad. I pray that you now remove from me every

single defect of character which stands in the way of my useful-
ness to you and my fellows. Grant me strength, as I go out from
here, to do your bidding. Amen.

Eleventh Step Prayer (Prayer of St. Francis of Assisi)

Lord, make me a channel of thy peace—that where there is
hatred, I may bring love—that where there is wrong, I may
bring the spirit of forgiveness—that where there is discord,
I may bring harmony—that where there is error, I may bring
truth—that where there is doubt, I may bring faith—that
where there is despair, I may bring hope—that where there are
shadows, I may bring light—that where there is sadness, I may
bring joy. Lord, grant that I may seek rather to comfort than to
be comforted—to understand than to be understood—to love,
than to be loved. For it is by self-forgetting that one finds.
It is by forgiving that one is forgiven. It is by dying that one
awakens to eternal life. Amen.

Remember, that if you are uncomfortable with language that
includes the word *God,* you can always substitute the words *Higher*
Power, Source, Divinity, Nature, or whatever works for you.

Writing

I like to keep a journal on my nightstand. You can write out
prayers, intentions for the day, reflections on the previous day, or
thoughts about a reading. You can do this at any time from the

moment your eyes open right on through your practice. Use your journal to jot down thoughts or insights that arise during your meditation. If you are new to meditation, you can keep a pen and paper nearby to write down persistent to-dos that might nag at you when you meditate. This saves you from having to stop or keep lists in your head and lets you return to your practice.

Smiling Meditation

After you notice your first thoughts, breathe deeply, close your eyes, and smile gently—a half smile. Take a moment to note the feeling a smile generates. Let this feeling radiate through your body, so your whole being feels as if it is smiling. Something as simple as a smile can create *joy without cause*. This small shift can propel your day in a positive direction. Your whole body says, *Ah, this feels nice*. It only takes a few seconds, but serves as a powerful reminder of who you are as your day begins. Take another deep breath and open your eyes. You can return to the smiling meditation at any point in the day.

The One-Minute Meditator

This is a quick and easy meditation that reconnects you to yourself and your higher power. It is a body scan that is centering and relaxing. If you are waking up, you can sit at the edge of your bed. If it is later in the day, use a chair or lie on a mat. If you're at work, an office chair is fine.

Put on a half smile and close your eyes, paying attention to any tension in your body. Take a deep breath and move your awareness into the crown of the head. Gradually move your focus down to your forehead and temples, cheekbones and jaw. Now to your neck and shoulders, throat, chest, upper back, and upper belly. Your elbows and your wrists. How do they feel? How about your lower belly, lower back, and hip joints? If you notice any tightness or restriction there, move your awareness there, breathe in and out, and release any tension.

Next, move your awareness into your thighs, knees, calves, shins, ankles, and feet. Shift your attention back to your elbows, wrists, and fingers. As you move your mind's eye through the body, continue to check in to see if you're tense, stiff, or sore. Again, breathe in and out to release any holding. End with another deep breath. Smile.

This is a fast way to let go of stress and move inward. This simple meditation empowers you to take responsibility for the direction of your day. I recommend doing it several times a day, especially when dealing with an unpleasant situation or uncomfortable feelings. The One-Minute Meditator is your tool for staying in bliss no matter what happens. If you take just one minute to turn inward, you can prevent your whole day from slipping down the drain.

Five-Minute Meditation: The Wheel

If you are just waking up, keep a mat next to your bed and slide onto it (a hard surface is preferable to a mattress). Take a minute to check in with your thoughts and feelings. Cultivate an inner smile and begin a few gentle stretches—*any* stretches that feel good. Prana will tell your body how to manufacture these moves. As we often say, "Let the yoga do the yoga" while you observe. (If you continue this practice, you'll find that you create stretches and postures you never knew existed.)

Next, move to a chair or cushion. You can sit in a cross-legged (lotus) position or not, but you should find a comfortable pose that allows you to keep a straight spine. Place your attention at the sixth chakra—the seat of knowledge—located between your eyebrows.

Draw your attention to the tip of the nose where you can feel the subtle sensations of breath entering and leaving your body. Follow the full duration of the inhalation until you feel the breath flip over at the top, where it is neither an inhalation nor an exhalation. Then follow the full duration of the exhalation until it is neither an inhalation nor an exhalation. Silently witness the in-and-out pattern of your breath. As you witness this quiet rhythm, take a moment to experience that you are a human *being*.

Pay attention to these moments between breaths. Feel the relaxation that this practice brings as you put your breath on a wheel—inhalation connecting to exhalation, over and over again. Notice your belly rising and falling. Every time you slip off to a thought, emotion, or feeling, simply note it, and gently escort your mind back to the next inhalation. Your breath will put you back in the moment. If thoughts arise, remember they are part of the process, part of being human. Learn to release and relax the body on each exhale as well.

After a few minutes, return to a standing position and move into the forward bend. Hang there for a few seconds. Be sure to maintain a slight bend in the knees. Roll up very slowly, starting with your lower back, following your awareness and continuing to move slowly up through your shoulders and neck. Bring your awareness to the mind's eye at the center of the forehead and check in with your feelings for a moment.

End by giving thanks for the gifts of your body and breath. Move about your morning.

Note: The Wheel can be practiced for much longer periods; however, five minutes is enough to reap benefits from this wonderful meditation. It is particularly useful after postures or breathwork to help integrate their effects.

Fifteen-Minute Meditation

• Complete Yogic Breath With Movement (seven times)
• Sun Salutation (three times)
• The Wheel (five minutes)
• Mantra Meditation

ALTERNATE: Guided Meditation #1 (fifteen minutes)

Thirty-Minute Meditation

• Complete Yogic Breath With Movement (seven times)
• Sun Salutation (three times)
• Basic Yoga Sequence

• The Wheel (five minutes)
• Sounding Breath (*Ujjayi*)
• One-Minute Meditator (Body Scan)

ALTERNATE: Guided Meditation #2 (thirty minutes)

Forty-Five Minute Meditation

• Complete Yogic Breath With Movement (seven times)
• Sun Salutation (seven times)
• Basic Yoga Sequence
• Fire Breath/Quick Outward Sniffs (*Kapalabhati*)
• Mantra Meditation

Or,

• The Wheel (fifteen minutes)

One-Hour Meditation

• Complete Yogic Breath With Movement (seven times)
• Sun Salutation (seven times)
• Basic Yoga Sequence
• Sounding Breath (*Ujjayi*)
• Fire Breath/Quick Short Sniffs (*Kapalabhati*)
• Alternate Nostril Breath (*Anulom Viloma*)
• Spinal Breath
• Guided Meditation #2

Or,

• The Wheel (thirty minutes)

Ninety-Minute Meditation

- Complete Yogic Breath with Movement (seven times)
- Sounding Breath (*Ujjayi*)
- Fire Breath/Quick Short Sniffs (*Kapalabhati*)
- Alternate Nostril Breath (*Anulom Viloma*)
- Sun Salutation (seven times)
- Basic Yoga Sequence
- Spinal Breath
- The Wheel (thirty minutes)
- Walking Meditation (fifteen minutes)

Two-Hour Meditation

- Complete Yogic Breath With Movement (seven times)
- Sun Salutation (seven times)
- Walking Meditation (thirty minutes)
- Sounding Breath (*Ujjayi*)
- Fire Breath/Quick Short Sniffs (*Kapalabhati*)
- Alternate Nostril Breath (*Anulom Viloma*)
- Spinal Breath
- Deeper Harmony (*Yoga Nidra*)
- Guided Meditation #1

Or,

- The Wheel (fifteen minutes)

INNER HARMONY EXERCISE

Prayer Wheel Exercise

A prayer wheel is a spinning cylinder inscribed with a mantra or prayer. Buddhists use prayer wheels to meditate and focus on the meaning of a given prayer, contemplating it each time it rotates into view. You are going to create your own metaphoric prayer wheel by choosing a prayer and then, over the course of a week, meditating on it using the different practices you've learned in this book.

What you need: a meditation cushion or chair, a yoga mat, your journal, and a pen.

What to do: Think up a prayer about a specific issue, concern, or question you have. Ask your higher power for guidance about this matter, then begin one of the meditation practices you've learned: sitting meditation, yoga, mantra, pranayama, or walking meditation.

Say the same prayer each day, but use a different form of meditation every time and notice whether any one practice seems to resonate with that particular prayer. Use your journal to record your thoughts, feelings, and impressions each day. You might discover that certain meditation practices are more effective with certain types of prayers. Use any information you glean from this exercise to help you choose which forms of meditation you want to use, and when, in your daily practice.

PART THREE:

Peace, Passion, and Purpose

11

KNOWING GOD'S WILL AND CARRYING IT OUT

*Once you understand the way life really works—
the flow of energy, information, and intelligence that
directs every moment—then you begin to see
the amazing potential in that moment.*

—Deepak Chopra

I DON'T KNOW.

These are three of the most powerful words in the universe. Within this simple statement lies the potential for anything to happen.

If you are sure what you want out of life, if you are certain where you want to go, who you want to be, and what you want to do, then you are bound by the limitations of your thinking. When you have all the answers you shut people out, ignore new ideas and information, and miss opportunities that might send you in a direction far better than anything you could have dreamed of.

I've told you about my own struggles with addiction, and how reconnecting to my authentic self and relying on my higher power for guidance and strength gave me enough trust to give up certainty about who I thought I was and how my life should look. It was then that I truly started to live my authentic life—a life full of surprises.

What Can You Expect?

How will the fruits of the Eleventh Step show up in *your* life? Should you pray and meditate then wait around for spiritual marching orders to arrive by e-mail? Can you expect, like Moses, to find two stone tablets on your doorstep with your life's purpose etched into them? Obviously not.

How can you feel secure enough to trade in your old ideas and values and give yourself over to something so intangible? How do you even know whether the direction you receive is coming from a power greater than yourself or is just your ego offering up more addictive thinking?

The truth is there are no clear answers, no absolutes. But when you practice the Eleventh Step regularly, when you quiet down and tune in, you start to feel truth in your bones. You become keenly aware of your motives. You know if you are acting out of fear, envy, and anger, or out of compassion, love, and kindness. You feel it energetically—by the way you hold tension in your body and how your breath changes.

Prayer and meditation clear the channels of your mind and heart, so your higher power can move and work through you. This does not happen magically. It is a connection—a partnership— you have to work at by staying spiritually fit. When you do this, your higher power meets you with energy and resources that help you access your highest potential. It is a spiritual dance of sorts, and your part is to stay honest, open, and willing.

Debtors Anonymous: Faith in Action

Let's look for a moment at Debtor's Anonymous (DA), a Twelve Step program that helps people stop using unsecured debt compulsively, often by addressing behaviors like overspending, underearning, and even workaholism. DA deals with money and livelihood issues, and as such, places a heavy emphasis on *action*.

I point to DA because, in addition to the Steps, this program offers members a powerful set of tools that helps them foster an active partnership with their higher power. The tools help members take full responsibility for their finances and work lives, while surrendering to the guidance, wisdom, and strength of a higher source. These tools include meetings, record keeping, sponsors, pressure relief groups, spending plans, action plans, the phone and Internet, DA and AA literature, awareness, business meetings, service, and anonymity.

I won't go into detail about each of the tools (you can find out more about them through the Resources section of this book), but suffice it to say they offer concrete ways to *suit up and show up* with lots of help. The DA tools balance practicality with humanity and spirituality; earthly concerns with divine inspiration. DA members are encouraged to use these tools regularly. There is a slogan DA members sometimes use that embodies the sprit of the tools and the partnership they seek to foster with a higher power: *Take the action, let go of the result.*

This slogan is a powerful directive for anyone in recovery. If you move forward in faith and trust, if you take actions grounded in spirituality, connected to a higher power, you might not see the results you *want,* but you might get the results you need.

What About My Hopes and Dreams?

Many people ask, "If I turn over my will and life to the care of God as I understand him, will I have to give up all my hopes and dreams?!" No. But you should know that as consciousness deepens, your hopes and dreams often change because old desires no longer hold the same meaning. Sometimes dreams stay the same, but your motivation for pursuing them comes from an entirely different place. Be ready for anything. This is what comes with the territory of *I don't know.*

This has been true for me and for many men and women I have met who are committed to consciousness and growth. I have heard accounts of how they followed their inner wisdom only to discover entirely new dreams and goals. Soon, they met people they would have had no reason to know before. They traveled to places they'd never thought of visiting, had unexpected life-changing experiences that would have been outside the realm of possibility before.

Synchrodestiny

Deepak Chopra calls such life-changing and seemingly coincidental events *synchrodestiny*. The more attuned we become to divinity within, the more often these moments occur, he says. This has certainly been the case in my life. I used to chalk up many such coincidences to chance until a clear pattern emerged and I could see that I was being led in new directions. Soon, I began to expect such events, and I now understand that they are a natural extension of my spiritual journey.

The more I align with my higher purpose, the more resources start to come my way. Is this really a coincidence? I do know that the quality of my interactions has shifted dramatically. Today, I strive to bring love and service to my personal and professional relationships, rather than expectation and demands.

I know that this is a powerful attitude. Kindness, love, and compassion carry a high spiritual frequency. People respond strongly to these qualities, whether they are aware of them or not. Positive spiritual energy travels quickly from one person to another; it can reach far and deep into a family, business, or community.

One can never know exactly how karmic dots connect, but I do know that the universe now meets me in unexpected ways. For example, often when I set an intention to finish a project, the one person who knows how to help me shows up. Perhaps a friend introduces me to her, or a book she's written falls off my shelf, or she phones.

There have been times when I am awestruck by the way one thing leads to another. Years ago, I had heard about a workshop with Andrew Weil, the medical doctor who pioneered integrative medicine in the United States. From that workshop, I ended up traveling to Africa with him and studying with him. His work has had a profound influence on my own life and work. I remember being particularly amazed when he asked me to be chairman of the board of the National Integrative Medicine Council because the simple act of enrolling in a workshop had led me to that moment.

In fact, I was so shocked by the offer that my first reaction was to turn it down. "Andy," I said, "This isn't me. I'm not a *Robert's Rules of Order* kinda guy." But Weil said that was precisely why he wanted me in the post. He was looking for someone with fresh eyes, someone not steeped in the established ways of doing things.

At one point, Weil asked what my "platform" was. "My what?" I asked. I had no idea what he was talking about. But when he explained that my platform was my philosophy, what I hoped to accomplish, the words rolled off my tongue: "I want to effect change in politics, healthcare, and religion." Of this I was certain. I knew I had to accept. *Boom.* The universe had put me in the perfect position to do what was most important to me. Though I felt that I was in over my head at times, I knew I had been put there for a reason, and I worked hard to implement change.

There have been more of these amazing opportunities than I can recount, like being invited to be the United States liaison to the Global Holistic Health Summit in Bangalore, India. Among the most astonishing honors in my life was to go from being a student of the Dalai Lama to being asked by the Smithsonian Institute to cosponsor His Holiness's trip to Washington, D.C., and then receive his private blessing.

Of course, these are the most striking events. Synchrodestiny happens all the time and in far less monumental ways. The perfect space shows up for a yoga class. I am looking for a qualified practitioner for one of my wellness centers, and someone makes a recommendation without being asked.

These days, I am rarely anxious about how projects will come together. I trust that when I put one foot in front of the other, when I stay open, everything will work out. Rarely am I disappointed, and rarely do things turn out exactly the way I had planned.

INNER HARMONY EXERCISE

A Synchrodestiny Tree

Deepak Chopra uses the term *synchrodestiny* to describe coincidental events that move a person's life in a positive direction. How has synchrodestiny played a role in your life? Chopra suggests picking a significant point in your life and tracing it back to one of these coincidental events to understand how synchrodestiny functions.

What you need: Your journal and a pen.

What to do: Think about something that's working in your life, that makes you happy. This can be a relationship, a job, a new home, volunteer work, a new sponsor. Write it down at the top of a page. For example, "I have a great job."

Now, try to remember how you got this job. Go back a year, two years, five years, or to any significant point that clearly set you on this path.

Under the words you wrote, draw something resembling a family tree. The next level down on the tree you could write, "got a promotion," under that "worked hard," under that "met with a mentor," "had a great job interview," "wrote a strong resume," "asked a friend to help me with my resume," or "read an ad for the job while reading an article on Internet." Trace your path back as many steps as you can, going down as many as ten levels.

Next, circle the events that *were not* in your control. Think about any coincidences or accidents that led to this event, and note how they moved you forward on your path. For example, "I ran into an old friend who told me about the job." Such events represent synchrodestiny at work in your life.

As you continue your prayer and meditation practice, you will notice moments of synchrodestiny come faster and more frequently. To demonstrate this, try drawing synchrodestiny trees every couple of months. You will realize that more and more coincidences are starting to affect your life for the positive. Certainly, you control most of the events that shape your destiny. You choose whom to call, what you want to do each day. But as you become more aligned with your true nature, the universe meets you where you are. People, resources, and information start to come into your life unexpectedly. Events and coincidences line up in bringing you closer to your true nature and your true purpose.

12

Overcoming Pitfalls on Your Spiritual Journey

*I wake up every day, right here, right in
Punxsutawney, and it's always February 2nd,
and there's nothing I can do about it.*

—Phil Connors (Bill Murray), *Groundhog Day*

I N THE FILM *GROUNDHOG DAY,* Phil Conners, a bitter, jaded weatherman played by Bill Murray, gets stuck in a time warp, doomed to relive the same mundane day over and over until he reexamines his life and opens his heart to love. Only then is he free to move forward.

The comedy probably became a classic because it so beautifully captures a profound truth about human nature and spirituality: Life's challenges return over and over again until we learn from them.

When you commit to recovery, you make a choice to face life's challenges head on. If you've been at it awhile, you might have already found relief from problems that once confounded you before sobriety or abstinence, but you have surely noticed that some troubles don't go away. People who irked you before irk you now. Problems you couldn't solve before are still daunting. In fact, some of your old demons might even come at you faster and more furiously.

As we've said, being on an honest spiritual path doesn't guarantee problems will go away, but it usually means your ability and skill at handling them will keep improving.

An Upward Spiral

Spiritual growth is often depicted as a spiral that rises upward. The spiral represents the way we circle back over the same issues and situations only to meet them on a higher plane each time. Many Indian traditions believe this pattern plays out in reincarnation, with the soul returning over and over again to learn karmic lessons that ultimately move us toward enlightenment.

As you engage in your daily spiritual practice, you will find that certain challenges in the practice itself show up over and over again. They might come in the form of physical pain or as judgments and negative thinking. Some people get frustrated repeatedly when they can't recreate a state of bliss. Still others of us have trouble handling plateaus, where nothing seems to change. And then there's the opposite problem. You can get so lost in spirituality that you lose interest in earthly matters and drop out of life. This is another surefire way to put the brakes on your spiritual development.

Any and all of these issues can derail a person's spiritual growth. What is important to remember is that these are the normal pitfalls of a spiritual journey. The trick is to learn from them and use them as tools of growth. Then, as in *Groundhog Day*, they lessen and often disappear so you can move on.

Common Pitfalls

As you become more adept at prayer and meditation, many challenges that made your practice difficult in the beginning no longer bother you. However, as you move into deeper levels of consciousness, sometimes old challenges return and new ones arise. Accepting that you will always deal with strains and struggles is part of spiritual growth. This is learning to accept life on life's terms. It can be helpful, however, to know in advance that there are some common pitfalls that can arise as you continue your spiritual journey. These are some of them:

Physical Pain

After years of poor self-care and stress caused by substance abuse or other self-destructive behavior, people in recovery often struggle with physical pain or discomfort. When you're in pain, it is challenging to focus on breathing techniques, mantra meditation, and yoga.

The Lesson: If you bring awareness, acceptance, and attention to physical discomfort, it starts to subside.

Bring your mind into the part of your body that hurts. Acknowledge the pain and accept its presence. Breathe into it. Notice the subtleties of sensation. If, for example, you have neck pain, where exactly do you feel it? At the base of your neck? Near your skull? What kind of pain is it? A dull ache or sharp feeling? Again, take a deep breath and breathe into it, doing your best to let go of tension or holding around the area.

Try not to judge the pain. Instead, think of it as intense sensation. Watch how it comes and goes, builds and ebbs. See if the sensation has a center, whether it radiates up, down, or sideways. Continue to breathe in and out of the spot and notice if you are holding other parts of your body to try to compensate for the pain or block its intensity. Through mindfulness, you can merge with the sensation and understand it. Energy follows attention. Your focus will move healing energy where it is needed, and often the pain subsides.

Another option is to identify the chakra closest to the sensation then picture the color associated with it. (See Chapter 9.) Add the mantra that resonates with that center, chanting it aloud or hearing it in your head. If the pain is in an extremity, such as your foot, hand, or knee, focus on the chakra closest to the joint. Think about moving the color and sound right into the discomfort, releasing and relaxing on the inhalations and exhalations.

Yoga poses are another way to ease pain, and you can modify a pose, if necessary, to target the area in question. Accept where your body is, start where you can, then gently, slowly, extend past the edge of the sensation, all the while breathing into it, noticing how you feel, and being *very* careful to listen to your body's limits.

If you have serious, debilitating, or chronic pain, I suggest enrolling in one of the many mindfulness-based stress reduction programs now offered at hospitals around the country. You can find information about this in the Resources section of this book or on the Internet.

Negative and Judgmental Thoughts

When I first started meditating, I remember the freight train of negative thoughts that would rush through my head: *What are you doing sitting here wasting time? Ha! Look at you, trying to be spiritual. You're a terrible meditator. You'll never get it.*

The only thing that kept me going was trickery. The man who was to become my sponsor told me the white lie that everyone who participates in AA meditates thirty minutes a day. I believed him. I was so desperate to get well that I wanted to do it right. So, despite my endless bouts of frustration, impatience, and self-criticism, I stuck with it. I'm so glad I did.

The Lesson: Persistence, patience, and compassion. If you keep at it, you will learn to watch negative and judgmental thoughts go by and eventually they lessen.

I was told to have patience and compassion for myself. If I could do this, if I could give myself enough space to *do it all wrong*, I would become more skilled at seeing my thoughts with nonjudgmental awareness, and more easily be able to turn my attention back to my breath. When I gave myself room to be imperfect, it was much easier to detach from negative thoughts. No longer did I pack a bag and jump aboard the crazy-thinking train. I learned how to sit and watch it whiz by.

Eventually, I could quickly and easily move past the frustration of random, disparate, or negative thoughts. I remember finishing a meditation like this for the first time, marveling at how beautifully calm my mind had been. Which brings me to . . .

Clinging to the Pink Cloud

Once you experience the peace and bliss meditation can bring, there's a natural tendency to hang on to that feeling for dear life. Why wouldn't you? You've spent years in the misery of addiction, and then suddenly you're walking around in heaven. Everyone and everything seems beautiful. Life is perfect. Then one day, *bam*, something snaps you back to reality. You come crashing down faster than a clown in a dunking booth. Then, no matter how hard you try, you can't seem to get the bliss back.

In the grips of addiction, mood swings were the norm. Life was awful or beautiful, black or white. Shades of gray? What's that? There is a similar tendency when we pray and meditate to bring that mind-set with us, to swing from elation to frustration. Then you think, *If it can't be good all the time, what's the point?*

Some people get depressed and angry at this stage and give up.

The Lesson: You do not get to choose what you experience when you meditate, but you do get to choose how you react to it.

Spiritual growth is about balance and equanimity. While bliss is a wonderful state, it, like everything else in life, is temporary. If you try to cling to bliss, you are asking for a roller-coaster ride.

The lesson to be learned is to watch what your mind does. Be aware. Ride it out. Notice how and when your moods shift and say to yourself, *Huh, isn't that interesting?* When you stop trying to control the bliss, your experience of meditation evens out.

Plateaus

If you're getting bored with your practice or upset that your spiritual growth seems to be leveling off, it might be a sign that you have grown complacent or too certain about what you are doing. This is not the time to give up. My teacher, Yogi Amrit Desai, used to say, "If you're in balance, you're not doing the work." He did not mean we should live on an emotional roller-coaster, but that we should keep challenging ourselves, pushing slightly beyond our comfort zone whenever possible.

The Lesson: Seek out and be open to challenges.

When things get too comfortable, it can be a sign that you're playing it safe and avoiding challenges that make you evolve as a person. When you are immersed in spiritual growth, try not to rest on your laurels. Reach and stretch; take risks. Be willing to fail and make mistakes. This is living on the cutting edge, being a pioneer.

If you're truly following the divine charge you've been given, if you are living God's journey from the core of your being, then emotional risks are where you find growth. Yes, some of the things you try will not pan out, but some will—and when they do, take a deep breath and hold on to the bar because you are going to zoom ahead at light speed.

Dropping Out of Life

This was a big one for me. When I began my spiritual journey and experienced the incredible peace of mind that came with my newfound connection with a higher power, I wanted more. I dropped out of daily routines to pray, meditate, read, travel, and study with some of the world's great spiritual teachers. It was an amazing and profoundly beautiful period of my life that lasted for years, and I am grateful to have had the opportunity to immerse myself so totally in a spiritual lifestyle. I was lucky to have the resources to make such a commitment.

But as I went deeper into my practice the challenge of it lessened. It was much easier than playing the game of life. What I came to realize was that there are equally instructive, enriching paths that do not require the kind of solitude and total immersion that I chose. Toward the end of that period, I started to understand this intuitively, so when friends urged me to come back to the world to share what I had learned, I knew they were right. I could see there had been an equilibrium missing in my life, that it was time to face the lessons that being in the world and being of service bring.

The Lesson: Full engagement in life creates the highest opportunity for growth.

The true gifts of my journey came when I realized I could live in this world without having to swim in the muck and mire of the ego—the ping-ponging of judgment and the need to choose "for or against" that are the norms in society. I could be in the world without participating in all of its madness. More importantly, I could help to change it. That was not something I could do meditating in a cave.

I still love spending hours, even days, in meditation. I can easily sit on my porch from sunrise to sunset, bathing in stillness and silence. But I know I have important work to do. I use meditation and prayer for renewal, so I can go out into the world and experience the bliss that comes from service and bringing about constructive change.

If you find yourself wanting to check out, be honest with yourself. Ask if you are running away from life or taking time to become centered so you can face it head on.

Judging Others

Once you experience the sense of peace and emotional stability that comes from practicing prayer and meditation on a regular basis, other people's anxieties, fears, neuroses, and general lack of centeredness start to stand out in painful relief. Their energy can feel erratic and difficult to tolerate. At this point, it is easy to get frustrated with other people's shortcomings. Judgments and comparisons kick in: *I am so much more spiritual than she is. I keep telling my sponsee to pray and meditate, but he won't listen. My child is not seeing his behavior as clearly as I do.*

The Lesson: When you notice yourself judging other people's spiritual progress, it is a sure sign that your own spiritual practice needs work.

In Twelve Step programs we are often admonished not to "take someone else's inventory," a reference to the detailed introspection we are asked to undertake for ourselves in Step Four. It means it is not our job to gauge or analyze someone else's spiritual progress. Yes, it is human nature to judge and compare. And no, you are not bad for doing it. But when this happens, instead of buying into your annoyance and frustration, let your judgment serve as a signal that something is off balance in your own spiritual work.

The people in our lives serve as mirrors of our own issues. Ask yourself whether the person whose behavior irritates you is reflecting back something you don't like about yourself. If they are negative and critical, where in your life are *you* still negative or critical? If they are afraid to take risks, where are you afraid to take risks? And so on.

It is also helpful to remember that each of us is on his or her own spiritual path, and that you most likely cannot see the larger picture in another person's life. Yes, you can share your experience, strength, and hope, but if someone doesn't appreciate it or choose to act on your advice, let it go. Smile. Know that your words of wisdom might not be right for this person at this time. Perhaps he or she might not be capable of hearing you *today,* but your words could ring true tomorrow, the next day, or five years from now. Bless the other person and be grateful they are on a spiritual path at all. To quote another popular Twelve Step slogan: Live and let live.

As you can see, being skilled at prayer and meditation does not guarantee your spiritual journey will be easy. A lesson to take away can be summed up in yet another popular slogan: Awareness, Acceptance, Action (the Three As). Be *aware* that it is easy to fall into traps as you work to align yourself with a higher power and your true nature. *Accept* that you will probably never be perfect, and that there will always be spiritual challenges to overcome. And take whatever *action* is necessary to change your attitude and behavior. This is the formula for spiritual growth.

INNER HARMONY EXERCISE

Groundhog Day

What problems repeat in your life, won't budge? We all have persistent issues that run through our lives like a bad theme song. How can you move beyond them?

What you need: Your journal, a pen, a timer.

What to do: Think about a problem that has been with you for many years. For example: *I can't get along with my mother. I get into arguments at work. I never finish what I start.* Write down five separate events in which the problem was most destructive. Set the timer for five minutes and write without stopping.

When you are done, reread what you have written and circle anything that involves blame. This will usually involve words like "he did," "she made me," and so on.

Now, replay the situation in your head, but this time imagine that the other person was completely helpless to act differently, that they were reading a script, and the only person with any power to change the outcome of the situation was you.

What could you have done differently? Could you have held your tongue? Left the room? Shared your feelings? See if you can come up with at least one thing that was in your control that could have shifted the energy of the situation, changed someone's mind, or simply eliminated the conflict all together.

If you cannot think of anything, that is okay, too.

Do three complete yogic breaths (see page 169) to clear your mind and body of any stress or tension that might have arisen as a result of this exercise.

13

SPIRITUAL AND SOCIAL EVOLUTION

While our ancestors knew of only one true way,
we have a cornucopia of spiritual and psychological
and physical possibilities.

—Paul H. Ray and Sherry Ruth Anderson

FTER YEARS OF FOCUSING INWARD, I find that my attention is increasingly turning outward. I eagerly seek out new ideas, philosophies, and methods to improve programs at my Inner Harmony Wellness Centers, Inner Harmony Yoga School, and educational outreach programs. I am exploring alternative models of addiction treatment at the Integrative Life Center, an outpatient facility that I recently cofounded in Tennessee with recovery pioneer Lee McCormick.

I have come to take very seriously Mahatma Gandhi's exhortation to "be the change you want to see in the world." I believe it is my responsibility to help move society in a positive direction. I also believe that anyone committed to spiritual growth eventually feels that way, too. With that in mind, I am drawn to the visionary work of several philosophers, spiritual leaders, writers, and psychologists whose ideas about the mechanics of cultural and social change resonate closely with insights I have gleaned through prayer and meditation.

I share their ideas with you because I believe their wisdom can spark change on the planet. These scholars have given me a clearer understanding of the nature of consciousness, how it expands and contracts on an individual, cultural, societal, and global level. It is my hope that these ideas will interest you, motivate you to think on a large scale as well, and inspire you to "be the change you want to see in the world."

Exploring Human Consciousness

Sri Aurobindo; Abraham Maslow, Ph.D.; A. H. Almaas; Ken Wilber; Steve McIntosh; Paul Ray, Ph.D.; and Sherry Ruth Anderson, Ph.D., have explored the role consciousness plays in individual, cultural, and social change. Their work examines human interaction, not through a lens of right and wrong, black and white, positive and negative (a view prevalent in media and culture), but as an extension of evolving consciousness. Together, their views have inspired or are key to a movement called Integral Philosophy.

The Integral point of view is that individuals, cultures, and social systems function at varying levels of consciousness. However, some societies and cultures are more conscious than others. Nonetheless, cultures and societies that operate at lower levels of consciousness should be "included" (not rejected) by societies and cultures at higher levels. By doing this, the groups at both levels of consciousness can "transcend" to higher states of awareness. To me, this model is akin to that of the Twelve Steps, which asks people with more recovery to accept those with less, then "include" them in their journey through the Steps. Through this acceptance, both the new and more experienced people grow spiritually and "transcend" to a higher level of consciousness.

This attitude of tolerance and compassion goes beyond "them and us" thinking. I believe this is a model that can shift the collective consciousness of the planet. In a nuclear age, this is surely a better way to bring about change than waging war.

Consciousness and Change

It is not hard to see how consciousness plays a vital role in social and cultural change. Fifty years ago an African-American man would not have been allowed to eat in some restaurants or to sit at the front of a bus. Today Barack Obama is president of the United States. This change happened through the tireless struggle, determination, and sacrifice of hundreds and thousands if not millions of men and women on several continents. But like any revolution, this enormous change began with a shift in consciousness among a few individuals.

Similarly, environmental awareness has exploded over the past fifty years. There are higher auto-emission standards and tighter regulations on industrial waste. The U.S. Congress recently approved legislation that paves the way for the first wind farms to be built off the coast of Massachusetts.

Of course, the world has a long way to go when it comes to race relations and environmental issues, but you'd have to be a hardened cynic to deny that society is far more tolerant of individual differences and far more aware of the planet's limited resources than it was only a half-century ago.

Seven Levels of Consciousness

To understand Integral Philosophy, it helps to explore consciousness itself. *Webster's New World Dictionary* defines "consciousness" as *awareness of one's own feelings, what is happening around one.*

According to many Eastern traditions, the human mind has the capacity to experience consciousness on seven levels. These are:

1. Sleeping—A state of minimal awareness or thought.
2. Dreaming—A state in which the mind is active, though mainly in response to inner stimuli.
3. Waking—A state in which our thoughts and feelings respond to our own ideas and to stimuli from the outside world. This state encompasses varying degrees of understanding and wisdom.
4. Pure Consciousness—A state in which the mind is mostly quiet, but able to witness sensation, thoughts, and ideas as they come and go.
5. Cosmic Consciousness—A state in which there is a sense of profound peace and acceptance, with the understanding that positive

and negative states are inseparable—that is, are two sides of a whole.

6. Divine Consciousness—A state in which we have the ability to recognize divinity in all things and beings.

7. Unified Consciousness—This is the state of enlightenment, in which there is an ongoing understanding of the true nature of existence and the realization that there is no separation between us and the universe: We are part of everything.

Integral philosophers draw from this kind of model, understanding that consciousness is not static and that it is possible for individuals and groups to ascend to the highest levels.

Divine Life on Earth: Sri Aurobindo

Much of the work in the Integral movement springs from Indian yogi, poet, and philosopher Sri Aurobindo, who understood and experienced all the states of consciousness before he died in 1950. He believed that the highest level of consciousness, which he called "Divine life on earth," is attainable and within reach. However, he suggested that it takes time to achieve such states and that, especially in culture and societies, they are arrived at through a process similar to human evolution. It may take time to get there, he believed, but global human consciousness is heading in an upward direction.

Hierarchy of Needs: Abraham Maslow

At about the same time Aurobindo taught, American psychologist Abraham Maslow postulated that human consciousness is affected by a "hierarchy of needs." Maslow believed people advance through higher states of consciousness and self-realization as their needs are met at successively higher levels. Maslow described the five levels of human need as:

1. Physiological: the need for nourishing food, clean water, warmth, sex, sleep, and health.
2. Safety: the need for safe, secure housing; economic stability; and the ability to fend off attacks.
3. Love and belonging: the need for family, friends, community, social acceptance, and emotional and sexual intimacy.
4. Self-esteem: the need for respect, support, confidence, and achievement.
5. Self-actualization: the need for morality, creativity, problem-solving, acceptance, and open-mindedness.

The Diamond Approach to Higher Consciousness: A. H. Almaas

Building on Maslow's ideas, author and teacher A. H. Almaas developed the Diamond Approach, a method of personal exploration and self-inquiry rooted in psychology, spirituality, and Socratic dialogue. Almaas's method uses a line of psychological and spiritual questioning designed to peel away layers of the ego and false self. The process shines light on outworn habits and beliefs born of unmet needs. This is said to remove psychological and spiritual blocks to a person's true and many-faceted nature. Through this practice, the individual attains higher states of consciousness, which paves the way for self-realization.

Transcend and Include: Ken Wilber

In another model, modern-day writer and philosopher Ken Wilber, considered the pioneer of the Integral movement, explores the way human consciousness changes and grows at the level of the individual, culture, and social structures. He believes that all of these structures are interrelated, that consciousness can remain static in some areas while advancing in others in a constantly shifting pattern, and that this can all take place at once. The ultimate result is a general trend toward higher consciousness for all.

It is Wilber who coined the term "transcend and include," asserting that it is important to "embrace and enfold" lower levels of consciousness into higher levels, so that higher levels of consciousness can emerge and move toward something nearing Aurobindo's "divine life on earth."

Levels of Human Development: Steve McIntosh

Steve McIntosh, author of *Integral Consciousness and the Future of Evolution: How the Integral Worldview Is Transforming Politics, Culture, and Spirituality* (Paragon House, 2007), examines human consciousness as it is reflected in changing values, perspectives, leadership styles, and other criteria. He sees human evolution progressing through six distinct levels of social and cultural development. These are:

1. Tribal—reflected in clans, tribes, and children.
2. Warrior—reflected in street gangs, prisons, and the country of Afghanistan.
3. Traditional—reflected in traditional religions, conservatives, and military culture.
4. Modernist—reflected in corporations, democracies, and modern science.
5. Postmodern—reflected in critical academia, liberals, and the social structures of the Netherlands.
6. Integral—reflected in the concept of world federalism and flexible structures.

McIntosh believes that certain developmental levels (which represent states of consciousness) dominate each period in history, but like Wilber, he also asserts that all of these levels can function together at once and that higher levels of development can only become manifest if we "embrace and enfold" the level that came before it.

Cultural Creatives:
Paul H. Ray and Sherry Ruth Anderson

Sociologist Paul H. Ray and psychologist Sherry Ruth Anderson studied people who have moved beyond McIntosh's Traditional and Modernist levels into Postmodern and Integral consciousness. Ray and Anderson view these people as Cultural Creatives. This group is described as highly curious and concerned, as activists and volunteers. These are people who value nature, spirituality, social justice, self-expression, and peace, among other things.

Ray and Anderson believe that Cultural Creatives are a growing segment of the population. I agree, and I think this is due in no small part to the fallout from addiction on the planet and the role the Twelve Steps have played in stemming the problem and transforming consciousness. If you doubt this, watch television shows like *Oprah* and *Dr. Phil.* It is not unusual for them and their guests to utter Twelve Step lingo, whether or not they have ever set foot in an AA, NA, OA, DA, Al-Anon, or other meeting room.

As a person in recovery, you truly are at the cutting edge of consciousness, not necessarily by choice, but because it has become part of your survival. Prayer and meditation are your tools for moving up through the seven levels of consciousness, through the hierarchy of needs, through the levels of human development. Right there on your meditation cushion or yoga mat, you have the power to start great social change where you are. What will you do with that power?

INNER HARMONY EXERCISE

Transcend and Include

Ken Wilber believes that cultures and societies can "transcend" to higher levels of consciousness by "including" people with stark differences. Integral philosophy is about acceptance and transformation. Where in your life could you be more accepting of others? How might being open and understanding about their thoughts and ideas help you move to higher levels of consciousness?

What you need: Your journal, a pen, and a timer.

What to do: When we are on a spiritual path, we sometimes think of people who are not pursuing personal growth as somewhat less conscious or enlightened than we are.

Bring a person like this to mind. Someone you disagree with on one or many issues. This can be someone you know personally or a politician or other influential figure. Pretend you are a speechwriter for that person. You *have* to express his or her point of view. The issue is your choice.

Spend fifteen minutes writing in that person's voice. Even if you totally disagree with them, try to the best of your ability to see how they think and why they believe what they do. When you are done, check in with yourself about what it felt like to sit in that person's shoes for fifteen minutes. Ask yourself whether you have even an ounce more understanding or compassion for them than you did before.

If you still can't feel any kind of connection with this person, *make up* a reason why they might feel the way they do. For example, if you believe in gun control, and the person you disagree with belongs to the National Rifle Association, create a fictional history for them in which they felt their life was in danger and they believed they needed a weapon for self defense. Notice whether your feelings about a person shift if you can understand, even for a minute, where they are coming from. This ability to transcend and include lies at the heart of Integral philosophy and is a foundation all of us can use to build a more peaceful world together.

14

INNER AND OUTER HARMONY

*The best way to find yourself is to lose
yourself in the service of others.*

—Mahatma Gandhi

I HAVE EXPERIENCED ECSTASY. I have known bliss. I have felt God within. After that, there was only one thing left to do: *be of service.*

In service I have found a happiness that has dwarfed any state of nirvana or material success I have ever known. In service, I have seen the sparkle return to a woman's eyes after years of suffering. I have seen a prison inmate discover a sense of purpose. I've seen a smile light up the face of a teenager who forgot what joy is. In service I have felt worthy and worthwhile; it is a high like no other.

If you seek to improve conscious contact with a God of your understanding, if you pray only for knowledge of your higher power's will for you and the power to carry it out—if you practice the Eleventh Step—you will ultimately discover that God's will for you is the same as it is for me: *be of service.*

There is no big mystery here. No secret. In fact, this is the message of the Twelfth Step: *Having had a spiritual awakening as the result of these Steps, we tried to carry this message to [the person who suffers], and to practice these principles in all our affairs.*

The Real Mystery

The real mystery is *how* your higher power wants you to be of service in the world. How will a God of your understanding use your unique talents, gifts, drives, and traits to move you to higher states of consciousness so you can move humanity in a positive direction?

What path will you take? This is the beautiful mystery. This is your spiritual journey toward inner and outer harmony.

When you create a clear, open channel to your higher power, the God of your understanding can move you past the excruciating emotional and spiritual pain that led you into addiction in the first place. People and resources will arrive to help you; you will indeed find the freedom and happiness you've been promised.

A Prayer to Be of Service

When you pray each day, ask your higher power how you can be of service. Ask for strength to act on whatever guidance you receive. Pray that you learn to recognize which of your skills and qualities can benefit people in need. Ask if your life experience can give someone else hope. Certainly, there is no lack of people in recovery or out who need your help.

Stay open to opportunities to be of service. Look close to home. Does someone in your family need to talk through a problem? Is there an elderly person in your neighborhood who needs help buying groceries? Maybe your boss could use assistance on a project.

There might be a young mother in your building who needs a babysitter for an hour or two. At your meeting, can you arrange chairs or sell literature? Can you give someone your phone number? These are simple acts of kindness that you can extend whether you are a CEO, a student, a housewife, or a laborer.

Start small. Bring someone a cup of coffee. Even the simplest gestures of kindness can reverberate long after you have offered your help. As you continue down your spiritual path, the desire to be of service will grow. Your higher power will call you to bring your unique set of life experiences, perceptions, and ideas to the people and situations around you. You will feel called to be of service in ways you never imagined.

You Matter

If you've lived with addiction for some time, you have likely become isolated. Often, with isolation comes a belief that you are unworthy of love and admiration. Maybe friends, relatives, or coworkers have grown to mistrust you, sometimes for real reasons. People have pulled away from you.

Service is a way to reconnect with people and establish trust. Even if you do not give directly to someone you know, your service to others demonstrates that you have integrity and are reliable. Your service shows people your willingness to give of yourself. These qualities are the currency of humanity; do not underestimate their value. No matter how sure you've become that you can't make a difference in someone else's life, or that you can't affect the world, think again. Your love, kindness, and compassion are more important than you probably realize. You matter.

The Seed of Change

Change begins with a commitment to stay connected to your higher power in each day. I have written many chapters stressing the importance of this one simple fact. In your commitment to spiritual growth lies the seed of change not only for yourself but for all humanity. Today, consciousness can evolve as fast as a message can ricochet around the globe on an iPhone. That is why, now more than ever, it is vital to think and act from your highest self.

Your journey to reconnect with your highest self, a journey to what Sri Aurobindo called "divine life on earth," begins in silence. In silence, you learn to be authentic and loving, kind and compassionate. In silence, you learn to find the truth and light your soul has been seeking. In silence you learn to be of service.

INNER HARMONY EXERCISE

Being of Service

If you attend a Twelve Step program you have likely taken on some kind of service commitment at a meeting, whether it is setting up chairs, being a treasurer, sponsoring, speaking, and so on. If you are not in one of the programs, perhaps you do volunteer work or help out friends and family members. Maybe you are not yet in a place where you feel ready to help anyone. It does not matter where you are on this spectrum. What matters is that you recognize that you have something to give.

What you need: a mirror, your journal, and a pen.

What to do: Look in the mirror for a minute or two. Look yourself in the eye and think about your strengths. These can be qualities such as kindness, compassion, understanding, or persistence. Or maybe you have a skill like cooking or playing the piano. Maybe you have some unusual ability, like being strong enough to move a piano. Write down everything you can think of.

Read over your list and use it to form a prayer. Take a deep breath and ask your higher power to use your skills and talents in service of others. Begin a five-minute Wheel Meditation (see pages 204–206). When you are done, take a long, deep breath. Write down any insights or guidance you received.

LOVING-KINDNESS
MEDITATION

AS YOU COMMIT TO THE ELEVENTH STEP and experience the joy, growth, and wisdom that will surely come as you seek guidance from a power greater than yourself, I leave you with a beautiful Buddhist prayer you can use before any meditation practice.

May I be well.
May I be happy.
May I be free of suffering.
May I love and be loved.
May I find the healing that I seek.
May I find peace.

Next, turn the prayer around and,
in service, give it away to others:

May you be well.
May you be happy.
May you be free of suffering.
May you love and be loved.
May you find the healing that you seek.
May you find peace.

Namaste,

Peter

THE TWELVE STEPS OF ALCOHOLICS ANONYMOUS

1. We admitted we were powerless over alcohol—that our lives had become unmanageable.

2. Came to believe that a Power greater than ourselves could restore us to sanity.

3. Made a decision to turn our will and our lives over to the care of God *as we understood Him.*

4. Made a searching and fearless moral inventory of ourselves.

5. Admitted to God, to ourselves, and to another human being the exact nature of our wrongs.

6. Were entirely ready to have God remove all these defects of character.

7. Humbly asked Him to remove our shortcomings.

8. Made a list of all persons we had harmed, and became willing to make amends to them all.

9. Made direct amends to such people wherever possible, except when to do so would injure them or others.

10. Continued to take personal inventory, and when we were wrong promptly admitted it.

11. Sought through prayer and meditation to improve our conscious contact with God, *as we understood Him,* praying only for knowledge of His will for us and the power to carry that out.

12. Having had a spiritual awakening as the result of these Steps, we tried to carry this message to alcoholics, and to practice these principles in all our affairs.

Copyright A. A. World Services, Inc.

RECOMMENDED READING AND LISTENING

Twelve-Step Literature

Al-Anon: *Paths to Recovery: Al-Anon's Steps, Traditions and Concepts*, Al-Anon Family Group Headquarters, Inc.

Alcoholics Anonymous: *Alcoholics Anonymous* ("The Big Book"), A. A. World Services.

Alcoholics Anonymous: *Twelve Steps and Twelve Traditions*, A. A. World Services.

Debtors Anonymous: *A Currency of Hope*, Debtors Anonymous.

Gamblers Anonymous: *Sharing Recovery Through Gamblers Anonymous*, Gamblers Anonymous.

Narcotics Anonymous: *Narcotics Anonymous*, Narcotics Anonymous World Service Office.

Overeaters Anonymous: *Overeaters Anonymous, 2nd Edition* ("The Brown Book"), Overeaters Anonymous, Inc.

Overeaters Anonymous: *Twelve Steps and Twelve Traditions of Overeaters Anonymous*, Overeaters Anonymous, Inc.

Sex and Love Addicts Anonymous: *Sex and Love Addicts Anonymous*, Augustine Fellowship.

Other Books

A. H. Almaas, *Facets of Unity: The Enneagram of Holy Ideas*. Berkeley, CA, Diamond Books, 1998.

———, *Diamond Heart Book (1): Elements of the Real in Man*. Berkeley, CA, Diamond Books, 1987.

———, *The Inner Journey Home*. Boston, Shambhala, 2004.

Sri Aurobindo, *The Life Divine*. Pondicherry, India, Sri Aurobindo Ashram Press, 1990.

Jill Bolte Taylor, *My Stroke of Insight: A Brain Scientist's Personal Journey*. New York, Penguin Group, 2006.

Joseph Califano, *High Society: How Substance Abuse Ravages America*. New York, Public Affairs, 2007.

Carlos Castaneda, *The Wheel of Time*. Los Angeles, La Eidolona Press, 1998.

Pema Chodron, *The Places That Scare You: A Guide to Fearlessness in Difficult Times*. Boston, Shambhala, 2001.

Deepak Chopra, *Buddha: A Story of Enlightenment*. New York, HarperOne, 2007.

———, *The Spontaneous Fulfillment of Desire*. New York, Harmony Books, 2003.

———, *The Path of Love: Renewing the Power of Spirit in Your Life*. New York, Harmony Books, 1997.

———, *Ageless Body, Timeless Mind: The Quantum Alternative to Growing Old*. New York, Harmony Books, 1993.

———, *Power, Freedom & Grace: Living From the Source of Lasting Happiness*. San Rafael, CA, Amber-Allen, 2006.

———, *The Seven Spiritual Laws of Success*. San Rafael, CA, Amber-Allen, 1994.

———, *The Seven Spiritual Laws of Yoga: A Practical Guide to Healing Body, Mind & Spirit*. Cowritten with David Simon. Hoboken, NJ, John Wiley & Sons, 2004.

Andrea Joy Cohen, *A Blessing in Disguise: 39 Lessons From Today's Greatest Teachers.* New York, Berkley Publishing, 2008.

Allan Combs, *Consciousness Explained Better.* St. Paul, MN, Paragon House, 2009.

Dalai Lama, *Kindness, Clarity, Insight.* Ithaca, NY, Snow Lion Publications, 1984.

John Davis, *The Diamond Approach: An Introduction to the Teachings of A. H. Almaas.* Boston, Shambhala, 1999.

Amrit Desai, *Kripalu Yoga: Meditation in Motion.* Lenox, MA, Kripalu Communications, 1984.

———, *Happiness Is Now: Reflective Writings.* Lennox, MA, Kripalu Communications, 1982.

———, *Amrit Yoga: Explore, Expand, Experience the Spiritual Death of Yoga.* Salt Springs, FL, Yoga Network International, 2000.

John English, *The Shift: An Awakening.* Phoenix, AZ, Dreamtime Publications, 2003.

Kahlil Gibran, *The Prophet.* New York, A. A. Knopf, 1923.

David Hawkins, *Power Versus Force.* Carlsbad, CA, Hay House, 2002.

Roger Jahnke, *The Healer Within: Using Traditional Chinese Medicine,* San Francisco, CA, HarperSanFrancisco, 1997.

Jon Kabat-Zinn, *Full Catastrophe Living: Using the Wisdom of Your Body & Mind to Face Stress.* New York, Delacorte, 1990.

Jack Kornfield, *A Path with Heart: A Guide Through the Perils & Promises of Spiritual Life.* New York, Bantam Books, 1993.

Steve McIntosh, *Integral Consciousness & Future or Evolution.* St. Paul, MN, Paragon House, 2007.

Dan Millman, *The Way of the Peaceful Warrior: A Book That Changes Lives.* Tiburon, CA, Publisher's Group West, 1984.

Thomas Moore, *Care of the Soul.* New York, Harper Collins, 1992.

Thich Nhat Hanh, *For a Future To Be Possible: Buddhist Ethics for Everyday Life.* Berkeley, CA, Parallax Press, 2007.

———, *Teachings on Love*. Berkeley, CA, Parallax Press, 1997.

———, *Interbeing: 14 Guidelines for Engaged Buddhism*. Berkeley, CA, Parallax Press, 1987.

———, *The Heart of Buddha's Teaching*. New York, Random House, 1998.

———, *Anger: Wisdom for Cooling the Flames*. New York, Riverhead, 2001.

———, *Joyfully Together: The Art of Building a Harmonious Community*. Berkeley, CA, Parallax Press, 2003.

Maharaj Nisargadatta, *I Am That: Talks with Sri Nisargadatta Maharaj*. Durham, NC, Acorn Press, 1999.

Helen Palmer, *The Enneagram: Understanding Yourself & Others in Your Life*. New York, Harmony Books, 1998.

Ravi Ravindra, *Science & the Sacred: Eternal Wisdom in a Changing World*. Wheaton, IL, Quest, 2002.

Paul Ray and Sherry Anderson, *Cultural Creatives*. New York, Harmony Books, 2002.

Richard Rosen, *The Yoga of Breath: A Step-by-Step Guide to Pranayama*, Boston, Shambhala, 2002.

Sri Sri Ravi Shankar, *Celebrating Silence*. Santa Barbara, CA, Art of Living Foundation, 2001.

Eckhart Tolle, *The Power of Now: A Guide to Spiritual Enlightenment*. Novato, CA, New World Library, 1999.

Neale Donald Walsch, *Tomorrow's God: Our Greatest Spiritual Challenge*. New York, Atria Books, 2004.

———, *Conversations with God Book 1: An Uncommon Dialogue*. New York, Putnam, 1996.

———, *Conversations with God Book 2: An Uncommon Dialogue*. London, U.K., Hodder & Stoughton, 1999.

Robert Walsh and Frances Vaughan, *Paths Beyond Ego: New Consciousness Reader*. New York, Putnam, 1993.

Andrew Weil, *Natural Health, Natural Medicine,* Boston, Houghton-Mifflin, 2004.

———, *8 Weeks to Optimum Health: A Proven Program for Taking Full Advantage of Your Body's Natural Healing Power.* New York, Random House, 1997.

———, *Natural Health, Natural Medicine.* Boston, Houghton-Mifflin, 2004.

Ken Wilber, *The Simple Feeling of Being: Embracing Your True Nature.* Boston, Shambhala, 2004.

———, *One Taste: The Journals.* Boston, Shambhala, 1999.

Marianne Williamson, *The Healing of America.* New York, Simon & Schuster, 1997.

Gary Zukov, *The Seat of the Soul.* New York, Simon & Schuster, 1989.

CDs and Downloads

Barry Bernstein, *Drone Tones.* Healthy Sounds.

Cosmic Energy, *Chakra: Meditation in Seven Parts.* Aquarius International Music.

Gary Edelberg, *Vibrational Healing/Lower Chakras.* Garye.

J. S. Epperson, *Higher* (Hemi Synch), Monroe Products.

Jonathan Goldman, *The Lost Chord.* Spirit Music.

———, *Chakra Chants.* Spirit Music.

Dr. Valerie Hunt, *Music of Light: The Only Authentic Auric Tapes.* Malibu Publishing.

Brian E. Paulson, *The Power of 7.* HealingProducts.com.

Layne Redmond, *Chanting The Chakras: Roots of Awakening,* Sounds True.

Robert Slap, *Eternal Om.* Valley of the Sun Publishing.

Deborah Van Dyke and **Valerie Farnsworth**, *Sound of Light: The Pure Tones of Crystal Singing Bowls.* Sounds of Light.

RESOURCES

Soul Silence
www.soulsilencethebook.com

**Inner Harmony Wellness
  Centers**
Scranton, PA
743 Jefferson Ave.
Mercy Hospital General Services
  Building, Suite 104
Scranton, PA 18510
Tel: 570-346-4621
www.innerharmonywellness.com

St. Maarten, Netherlands Antilles
Plaza Puerta del Sol
Welfare Rd. 68, Unit 212
Simpson Bay, St. Maarten,
  Netherlands Antilles
Tel: 011-599-581-5480
www.innerharmonywellness.com

Inner Harmony Yoga Institute
743 Jefferson Ave.
Mercy Hospital General Serviccs
  Building, Suite 104
Scranton, PA 18510
Tel: 570-346-4621
www.innerharmonyyogainstitute.com

Scranton Studio
UNO Fitness Center
3 W. Olive St., Suite 210
Scranton, PA 18508-2574
www.innerharmonyyogainstitute.com

St. Maarten Studio
Plaza Puerta del Sol
Welfare Rd. 68, Unit 304
Simpson Bay, St Maarten,
  Netherlands Antilles
Tel: 011-599-581-5480
www.innerharmonyyogainstitute.com

**Harmony Mountain
  Spa & Retreat**
743 Jefferson Ave.
Mercy Hospital General Services
  Building, Suite 104
Scranton, PA 18510
Tel: 570-346-4621
www.innerharmonywellness.com

Integrative Life Center
1104 16th Ave.
Nashville, TN 37212
Tel: 877-334-6958; 615-891-2226
www.integrativelifecenters.com

Arizona Center for
Integrative Medicine
P.O. Box 245153
Tucson, AZ 85724-5153
Tel: 520-626-6417
www.integrativemedicine.arizona.edu

The Chopra Center
2013 Costa del Mar Rd.
Carlsbad, CA 92009
Tel: 760-494-1600; 888.424.6772
Website: www.chopra.com

Esalen Institute
55000 Highway 1
Big Sur, CA 93920
Tel: 831-667-3000
www.esalen.org

Omega Institute
150 Lake Dr.
Rhinebeck, NY 12572
Tel: 877-944-2002
www.eomega.org

Amrit Yoga Institute
P.O. Box 5340
Salt Springs, FL 32134
Tel: 352-685-3001; 352-685-3002
www.amrityoga.org

Yoga Alliance
1701 Clarendon Blvd., Suite 110
Arlington, VA 22209
Tel: 888-921-YOGA (9642)
www.yogaalliance.org

Institute of Noetic Sciences
101 San Antonio Rd.
Petaluma, CA 94952
Tel: 707-775-3500; 877-769-4667
www.noetic.org

The Tibet Fund
241 E. 32nd St.
New York, NY 10016
Tel: 212-213-5011
www.tibetfund.org

Health Action
5276 Hollister Ave., #257
Santa Barbara, CA 93111
Tel: 805-617-3390
www.healthaction.net

Marworth Substance
Abuse Services
Lily Lake Rd.
Waverly, PA 18471
Tel: 570-563-1112, ext. 301
www.Marworth.org

Clearbrook Treatment Centers
Tel: 800-582-6241
www.clearbrook.org

Clearbrook Lodge
890 Bethel Hill Rd.
Shickshinny, PA 18655

Clearbrook Manor
1100 E. Northampton St.
Laurel Run, PA 18706

Insight Meditation Society
The Retreat Center
1230 Pleasant St.

Barre, MA 01005
Tel: 978-355-4378
www.dharma.org

**Kripalu Center
for Yoga & Health**
Stockbridge, Massachusetts
Tel: 866-200-5203
www.kripalu.org

**Center for Mindfulness in
Medicine, Health Care,
and Society**
55 Lake Avenue North
Worcester, MA 01655
Tel: 508-856-2656
www.umassmed.edu/cfm

Twelve-Step Programs
*Alcoholics Anonymous World
Services, Inc. (AA)*
Mailing Address:
P.O. Box 459
New York, NY 10163
Tel: 212-870-3400
Office:
475 Riverside Dr. at W. 120th St.,
11th Floor
New York, NY 10115
www.aa.org

*Al-Anon Family Groups
(Al-Anon)*
1600 Corporate Landing
Parkway
Virginia Beach, VA 23454-5617
Tel: 757-563-1600
www.al-anon.org

Narcotics Anonymous (NA)
P.O. Box 9999
Van Nuys, CA 91409
Tel: 818-773-9999
www.na.org

Overeaters Anonymous (OA)
Mailing Address: P.O. Box 44020
Rio Rancho, New Mexico
  87174-4020
Office: 6075 Zenith Court NE
Rio Rancho, NM 87144-6424
Tel: 505-891-2664
www.oa.org

Debtors Anonymous (DA)
P.O. Box 920888
Needham, MA 02492-0009
Tel: 800-421-2383; 781-453-2743
www.debtorsanonymous.org

Gamblers Anonymous (GA)
P.O. Box 17173
Los Angeles, CA 90017
Tel: 213-386-8789
www.gamblersanonymous.org

*Sex and Love Addicts Anonymous
  (SLAA)*
Fellowship-Wide Services
1550 NE Loop 410, Ste. 118
San Antonio, TX 78209
Tel: 210-828-7900
www.slaafws.org

INDEX

ABOUT THE AUTHOR

Peter Amato, M.A., is a psychotherapist, meditation master, and yoga instructor who has received certifications from Deepak Chopra, M.D., Jon Kabat-Zinn, Ph.D., and Yogi Amrit Desai. A student of world-renowned Buddhist monk, teacher, and Nobel Peace Prize-nominee Thich Nhat Hanh, he has also worked with and received private blessings from the Dalai Lama. Peter Amato is founder and CEO of the Inner Harmony Group, a Pennsylvania-based consortium of companies specializing in holistic health, addiction counseling, educational enrichment, personal growth, leadership development, and business consulting. His enterprises offer cutting-edge programs for individuals, corporations, academic institutions, and corrections facilities.